SCIENCE AND CRIMINAL DETECTION

Titles in the *Dimensions of Science* Series

DIMENSIONS OF SCIENCE
Series Editor: Professor Jeff Thompson

SCIENCE AND CRIMINAL DETECTION

John Broad

King's College
University of London

MACMILLAN
EDUCATION

First published 1988

Published by
MACMILLAN EDUCATION LTD
Houndmills, Basingstoke, Hampshire RG21 2XS
and London
Companies and representatives
throughout the world

Typeset by TecSet Ltd, Wallington, Surrey
Printed in China

British Library Cataloguing in Publication Data
Broad, John
   Science and criminal detection.—
   (Dimensions of science).
   1. Forensic science
   I. Title   II. Series
   363.2'5

ISBN 0-333-48325-1

To Steve, Graham, Marianne,
Vivien, Sue and Rajai

"Life is nothing but a competition to be the criminal rather than the victim."

Bertrand Russell

Contents

Series Editor's preface

This book is one in a Series designed to illustrate and explore a range of ways in which scientific knowledge is generated, and techniques are developed and applied. The volumes in this Series will certainly satisfy the needs of students at 'A' level and in first-year higher-education courses, although there is no intention to bridge any apparent gap in the transfer from secondary to tertiary stages. Indeed, the notion that a scientific education is both continuous and continuing is implicit in the approach which the authors have taken.

Working from a base of 'common core' 'A'-level knowledge and principles, each book demonstrates how that knowledge and those principles can be extended in academic terms, and also how they are applied in a variety of contexts which give relevance to the study of the subject. The subject matter is developed both in depth (in intellectual terms) and in breadth (in relevance). A significant feature is the way in which each text makes explicit some aspect of the fundamental processes of science, or shows science, and scientists, 'in action'. In some cases this is made clear by highlighting the methods used by scientists in, for example, employing a systematic approach to the collection of information, or the setting up of an experiment. In other cases the treatment traces a series of related steps in the scientific process, such as investigation, hypothesising, evaluation and problem-solving. The fact that there are many dimensions to the creation of knowledge and to its application by scientists and technologists is the title and consistent theme of all the books in the Series.

The authors are all authorities in the fields in which they have written, and share a common interest in the enjoyment of their work in science. We feel sure that something of that satisfaction will be imparted to their readers in the continuing study of the subject.

Preface

This short work does not pretend to be a comprehensive survey of the entire field of forensic science. It is an attempt to outline the scientific procedures that provide some of the facts presented as evidence at a court of law. The selection of topics obviously reflects the interests and inclinations of the author.

Clarity of expression is important to the forensic scientist. He or she may be required to explain to a jury the principles and practice behind the methods on which his or her findings are based.

The main purpose of the book is to be informative and scientific while, at the same time, being interesting and maybe thought-provoking. The last chapter on 'Crime and the Citizen' is intended as a basis for discussion.

Not all forensic work is exhilarating. Some is distinctly tedious and time-consuming with little, or no, apparent reward for effort. Direct contact with those working 'in the field', however, gives — to the author at least — a sense of enthusiasm and dedication that is more than impressive. No doubt this is one of the characteristics that the ordinary man or woman associates with the boffin.

Apart from those sufficiently interested to browse, the target reading group is the 16 to 18 year olds, who may need information about the world 'out there'. This book is largely based on talks that the author has given to various groups in schools and colleges. Hopefully it will prove useful to the casual reader, the future jurist and the budding scientist.

Acknowledgements

I would like to thank Ken Crear of the Metropolitan Police Forensic Science Laboratory for his assistance with the photographs, Richard Overill of King's College, London, without whose aid chapters 6 and 7 could not have been written, Tony Roberts of Farnborough Sixth Form College who started the ball rolling, my wife who read the typescript and corrected the many errors, and all those who gave help, words of advice and encouragement.

1   The Carnage on the Roads

Although violent crime makes headline news, the vast majority of the population do not experience it at first hand. Yet very few people escape direct experience of an incident involving a moving vehicle on the road. Accidents affect us all.

ALCOHOL AND ACCIDENTS

Well over 80 per cent of road accidents are caused by driver error and some authorities consider that over half of this 80 per cent is due to the effects of alcohol (chemically known as ethanol). Around midnight and into the small hours of the morning this half could increase to three-quarters. Behind these cold facts lies the emotional impact of personal involvement.

A few years ago the author's brother was driving off a dual carriageway in the late autumn evening. Suddenly he noticed some headlights approaching at speed and veering towards him.

> "Hardly before I realised it his wing ripped down the offside of my car. In a flash I was forced into the ditch and I heard an almighty crash behind me. Terrified I managed to get out and found a woman dead in the wreck of her Mini. The other driver was slumped over the wheel. As it turned out he was drunk but wasn't hurt because he was driving a big, heavy Rover. The dead woman I recognised as a neighbour with two children. She never stood a chance. It came out later that the fellow had three times the legal limit of alcohol in his blood. Another few inches, of course, and I would have been the one on the slab."

ALCOHOL IN THE BREATH

Roadside screening for alcohol (ethanol) in the breath can be carried out quickly by a number of devices. The police can stop and test anyone they suspect might be driving 'under the influence'. The flashing red light and the wave of the uniformed arm, followed by "Will you please blow into this sir?" is an all too common feature of modern affluent living.

Roadside screening devices are called breathalysers. One type is shaped like a balloon with a transparent mouthpiece. The driver blows into this mouthpiece, which contains yellow crystals of acidified potassium dichromate(VI). The alcohol (ethanol) in the breath changes the dichromate(VI) ion to green chromium(III) sulphate. It is the green colour that 'gives the game away'. Another screening device — the more modern Alcolmeter — works on the traffic light system; a green colour for negative, amber for on the borderline and red for positive. The coloured lights are situated on a pocket-sized black box into which the suspect blows. The positive red means that the breath contains more than the legal limit of alcohol (ethanol). The faster the red light appears the higher the alcohol level in the breath.

At present, in England, the limit is set at 35 μg per 100 ml of breath, or 35 μg%. This is likely to be reduced in the near future.

Legally acceptable evidence on the level of alcohol (ethanol) in the breath is gained from a machine called the Intoximeter — now standard equipment in Police Stations in England and Wales. The Camic Breathalyser is used in Scotland. Both have reduced the amount of forensic time devoted to drink/driving offences.

Breath blown into an Intoximeter is exposed to light from an infra-red source. At a certain wavelength — 3.2 microns — ethanol absorbs infra-red radiation. In accordance with the Beer–Lambert Law, this absorbance is directly proportional to the concentration of ethanol present.

Because the findings of an Intoximeter are allowed as evidence in a court of law, precautions have to be taken to ensure constant accuracy and instant precision.

In addition to two breath samples (a good deep blow), the machine is twice equilibrated with the background air (blanks) and twice standardised against an ethanol input of 35 μg% — the legal limit for driving a vehicle. A built-in compensation is made for the presence of propanone (acetone) that absorbs infra-red radiation in the ethanol range. The computer within

Figure 1.1 *The instrument of reckoning – the Lion Intoximeter 3000 (courtesy of Lion Laboratories Ltd).*
A *The breath inlet tube – a pullout, spring-loaded, tube into which the driver blows. The disposable mouthpiece can be taken away as a memento of the occasion.*
B *The data emerging from the internal computer.*
C *A generator of standard alcohol (equivalent to 35 µg alcohol per 100 ml of breath) can be attached to this side.*

the machine records all the information and the 'read out' is completed with the relevant signatures.

A person can, of course, refuse to blow into an Intoximeter; in fact he or she can refuse to comply with any request made by the police. However, such a course of action lays one open to prosecution – in this instance for 'failure to provide a sample'. Also any such refusal makes an unfavourable impression on a magistrate or a jury.

If an Intoximeter records two readings in the range 35–50 $\mu g\%$, then blood samples may be taken as further evidence. Usually the person being prosecuted requests a confirmatory blood test. The suspect, in English law, is given every chance and the benefit of any doubt goes his or her way. Very small amounts of blood are needed for forensic analysis: 5 ml are taken from a vein by a police surgeon and divided into two vials which are sealed. One vial is sent to the laboratory and the other can be used by the suspect for private analysis.

3

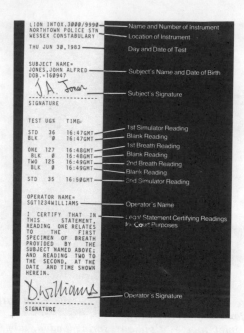

Figure 1.2 *The incriminating evidence – a specimen 'read out' from the Lion Intoximeter (courtesy of Lion Laboratories Ltd).* *All readings are in micrograms of alcohol.*

THE BLOOD ALCOHOL LEVEL

In the laboratory, the blood is subjected to gas chromatography (see chapter 2). The small quantity of blood is warmed in a closed space and a few microlitres of the resulting vapour are injected on to the separating column. This is known as head space chromatography and does assume (correctly) that the concentration of ethanol in the vapour is directly proportional to the concentration of ethanol in the blood below.

Gas chromatography is an accurate system for separating the components of a mixture prior to identification. But the ethanol has already been identified and the problem is to find out, on a very small sample, exactly how much ethanol is present in the blood. To do this an internal standard (propan-2-ol or propanol) is injected along with the ethanol. The two components emerge, or are eluted from, the separating column at similar, but distinctly different, times. This means that their retention times are close but separate.

4

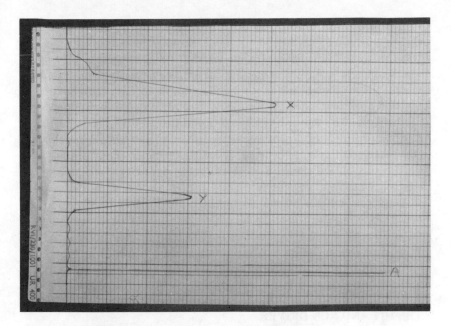

Figure 1.3 Alcohol in the blood.
A Gas Chromatograph (GC) 'read out'. Ten microlitres of gas above a specimen of blood containing alcohol was injected on to the column of the GC. This is better than injecting blood or serum on to the column.
The vertical, or y, axis is time in minutes. The time from A to a peak at X or Y is the retention time of either the Internal Standard or the alcohol. The x, or horizontal, axis represents the amount of the component leaving, or eluting from, the separating column.

The peak at Y is the one for ethanol. The peak at X is for the internal standard. The line A is the time of injection.

Accuracy and precision are important when measurement involves very small quantities. Precision means that a series of readings from an instrument are reliably constant and accuracy ensures that each reading is acceptably close to the correct, or true, value. If an instrument is accurate and also sensitive it has considerable scientific value. It is probably expensive into the bargain. Sensitivity implies that the detector within the machine responds to a low, or very low, concentration of a specific target substance despite the presence of background influences (or noise). Trained 'sniffer' dogs are sensitive to very low amounts of explosives in luggage, etc. A slight change in concentration brings a corresponding change in response from the instrument — and maybe from the dogs.

Chemical instruments, like writers, can be precise without being accurate.

In this case, when making use of an internal standard, accuracy requires prior construction of a standard curve. Known amounts of ethanol are injected on to the separating column with a standard amount of propan-2-ol. From the 'read outs' a graph is drawn. The increasing concentrations of ethanol are plotted as the x variable, with the corresponding ratios of the two peak heights as the y variable. The separate points are joined to form the standard curve. Using the ratios of the peak heights compensates for irregularities in the instrumental procedure. When a sample of unknown ethanol concentration is injected, the ratio of the emerging peak heights can be put on the standard curve. The corresponding concentration of ethanol can be read off directly.

The legal limit for ethanol in the blood (equivalent to 35 $\mu g\%$ in the breath) is 80 mg per 100 ml of blood, or 80 mg%. In Sweden this limit is set at 50 mg% and has been in force for much longer than in England. It is an offence against the law to drive a vehicle on the roads with more than the legal limit of alcohol (ethanol) in the blood.

THE HIT AND RUN DRIVER

One problem associated with the moving vehicle offence is the driver who rapidly leaves the scene of the accident. If there are no witnesses then tracing the car and its driver depends on the trace evidence left on the victim or other vehicles. Fragments of glass, bits of paint and marks can be left by the offending car. Evidence from a victim — fibres, blood, etc. — is only of use if the vehicle is found. Success in such cases depends upon a great deal of patient work plus a slice or two of luck.

If there are witnesses to a hit and run accident then the registration number can lead the police to the owner and probably the driver. Centralised computing facilities at Swansea allow rapid tracing of a car owner.

Sometimes the offending driver, aware that he or she might be 'over the limit' makes for home and rapidly swallows a number of stiff gins or their equivalent. This means that the police are confronted with a person who states that his or her high breathalyser result is caused by the intake at home. These attempts to cover up are known as after accident drinking or the 'Hip flask' defence. The question posed in these circumstances is — how much ethanol was in the person's blood at the time of the accident?

To provide an answer the clearance rate, or rate at which ethanol is eliminated from the body, must be known for the average individual. This can be done by experiments on volunteers — who are not difficult to find! A known amount of ethanol is swallowed over a specified time and the breath, blood and urine levels are monitored every 30 minutes.

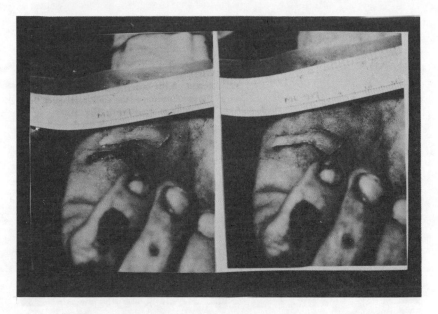

Figure 1.4 *A physical fit — literally! (copyright American Society for Testing and Materials — reproduced with permission).*
A portion of skin and flesh recovered from the fender of an automobile suspected of being involved in a hit and run incident. The 'item' fitted neatly into an injury sustained by the victim. Credit must be given to the alertness of the officer who spotted this piece of evidence — which really is damning!

One of the problems with ethanol experiments on volunteers is that conditions in the laboratory are nowhere near those 'out on the road'. The person who drives home for a quick drink or two is, in all probability, acting under the influence of high adrenalin. The laboratory experimenter does not have these effects.

CLEARANCE FROM THE BODY

Many factors are involved in the clearance of ethanol from the body. The first, obviously, is the initial dose and the spread of intake. The sex, health, build and weight of the individual are important. Fat distribution has to be taken into account. For the purposes of calculation these considerations are incorporated into the Widmark Factor, which determines the slope of

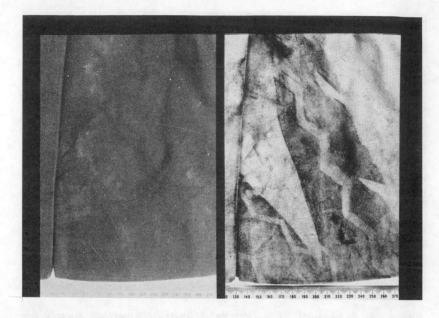

Figure 1.5 *The tread on the jacket (courtesy of the Metropolitan Police Forensic Laboratory).*
The left-hand side of the picture shows the back of a jacket in normal light. The wearer was run over in a hit and run traffic incident.
On the right-hand side is the same portion of jacket photographed when illuminated by infra-red light. The fabric of the clothing reflects the infra-red wavelength, whereas the dirt etc. absorbs it. A tyre mark shows clearly and this could give some clue about the automobile involved.

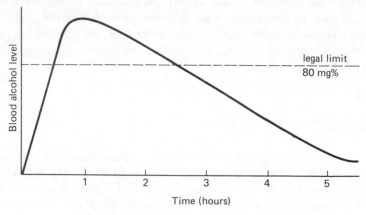

(a) Graph of intake over 30 minutes and subsequent clearance

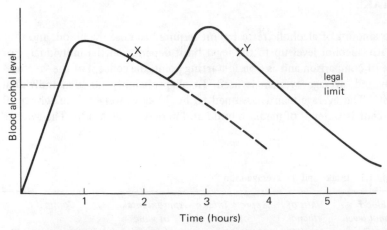

(b) As (a) but with later intake. If Y is the time when the blood alcohol level is monitored, what was the blood alcohol level at X — the time of the accident ?

Figure 1.6 *Graphs of intake and clearance of alcohol.*

the clearance line in figure 1.6. A straight line denotes that clearance is not dose related, so that a valid prediction about X may be made if Y is known.

Ninety five per cent of ethanol is dealt with by the liver and is changed to carbon dioxide and water. The remaining 5 per cent is eliminated in the urine and in the breath. The liver works at a constant rate and further ethanol intake does not speed up clearance. The extra ethanol takes longer to be eliminated from the body. The implication of this is that a person who enjoyed a good party into the small hours and was, sensibly, driven home by taxi, might be above the legal limit next morning when driving to work.

The average man clears ethanol from the body at the rate of 5 gm per hour or 15 mg per 100 ml of blood per hour. Many men will clear faster than this and some authorities think that 5 gm is on the low side. The average woman clears some 3 gm per hour or 9 mg per 100 ml of blood per hour. The average man can thus reduce a blood alcohol level of 100 mg% to 80 mg% in approximately 1.5 hours. The average woman would take over 2 hours to effect the same reduction. From 80 mg% back to normal would take the average man a further 5 hours and the average woman a further 8 hours.

INTAKE

The amount of alcoholic refreshment required to raise the blood, and thus breath, alcohol level up to the legal limit depends on the individual. For ease of comparison and as a basic starting point, the concept of the 'average' man and 'average' woman is used. In all probability no such individual exists. The average man is assumed to be 70 kg in weight — of which 70 per cent is water — of medium build and in reasonable health. The average

Table 1.1 Intake and the average man

Blood alcohol level (mg%)	Units of ethanol required	Approx. intake of beer (pints)	Approx. intake of wine (glasses)	Comment
80	4	2	4	At legal limit
160	8	4	8	Usual limit of social drinking
240	12	6	12	Approaching danger level
400	20	10 or 11	20	Probably unconscious

woman weighs in at 55 kg of which 55 per cent is water. Men are the leaner sex.

Assuming that ethanol is absorbed into the blood immediately and passed to the body tissues, the average man needs 4 units of ethanol to raise his blood level to 80 mg%. These 4 units can be provided from four tots of any spirit (70 per cent proof), or four normal glasses of vintage wine or two pints of standard beer. The number of units of ethanol present in a glass of home-made wine or in a tumbler of 'scrumpy' cider is open to conjecture.

On the same assumption, an average woman requires rather more than half the quantities needed by the average man. Strictly the assumption is not valid but it serves as a useful indicator. It in effect represents the 'worst possible case'. Alcoholic refreshment is seldom 'downed' all at once and most is accompanied by food, which slows absorption into the blood. While further ethanol is being consumed, the liver is busy eliminating that already in the body.

DRUNK OR SOBER?

The effects of ethanol on any individual depend on habit, intake and physical well-being. Even a small amount of ethanol affects the higher centres of the brain. The critical faculty is the first casualty and this leads to an increase in time taken to perform tasks requiring care and concentration.

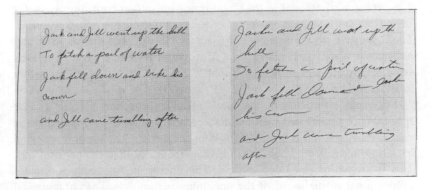

Figure 1.7 *Accuracy and alcohol.*
On the left is a nursery rhyme written by a person (assumedly an average drinker) with a blood alcohol level of zero.
On the right is the same nursery rhyme written by the same person, who now has a blood alcohol level just above the legal limit for driving, that is 80 mg%.
It is probable that a habitual drinker, with a tolerance to alcohol, would not show such a difference in legibility.

Despite the fact that alcohol is a powerful depressant of the nervous system, its first effects appear to be quite the reverse. Contrary to popular belief, ethanol is not an aphrodisiac. The initial stages of apparent stimulation are misleading.

> In fact ethanol hypes up the desire but progressively reduces the performance — eventually to the point of incapability.

The habitual drinker apparently suffers less from ethanol intake than the casual drinker. This is related to tolerance. Most people — the average ones — are rendered unconscious at 350–400 mg% of ethanol in the blood, but the heavy drinker might be still on his or her feet. The body adapts to regular ethanol intake although the liver can be under considerable strain.

SPEED AND ACCIDENTS

The presence of ethanol in the blood is one important contributory factor in moving traffic offences; the other is speed. Often the two go together. The aggressive driver is as big a menace as the drunken driver. After any multiple pile up, particularly on a Motorway, a Chief Constable reflects sadly, "Why are human beings so mad?" No one has yet come up with a satisfactory answer.

For rapid estimation of the speed of an approaching vehicle, a radar speed device can be used. This emits a radar signal which is directed at the vehicle moving towards the person holding the device. The signal is reflected back and this reflected signal has a higher frequency than the one sent out. This is known as the Doppler shift. This change in frequency is directly proportional to the speed of the oncoming automobile. The outgoing and incoming signals are compared and the frequency difference is automatically monitored as speed on a simple meter. Once again the familiar uniformed arm directs the motorist into the side of the road. The difficulty is that the radar beam spreads and can bounce off other objects, which may or may not be moving. Apparently one such device recorded a tree moving at 10 mph and a nearby house at 5 mph. Recently research has been commissioned into the substitution of a laser for the radar beam. This would prevent spread but the aim of the beam would have to be much more accurate.

THE MATHEMATICAL ASPECT

Car-to-car and car-to-pedestrian impacts often require a knowledge of the velocity at impact. This particularly applies if the incident occurred in a 30 or 40 mph speed limit zone. The calculation of the impact velocity involves the use of simple applied mathematics.

There are three equations of motion that connect speed (velocity), acceleration/deceleration, distance travelled and time.

$$v^2 = u^2 + 2as \qquad \text{(i)}$$

$$v = u + at \qquad \text{(ii)}$$

$$s = ut + \tfrac{1}{2}at^2 \qquad \text{(iii)}$$

In these equations, u is the initial velocity and the one that matters because it is the velocity at the moment of impact; v is the final velocity and is usually zero because the impact brings the vehicle to a halt; a is the acceleration/deceleration; and s is the distance travelled, which can often be revealed by skid marks. These are significant in the case of car-to-pedestrian impacts where the driver brakes to halt the car.

The most commonly employed equation is the first and in all of them, a (acceleration/deceleration) is assumed to be constant. The difficulty with trying to assess the velocity of a moving vehicle is that conditions vary. The road surface can be dry, wet or icy. The condition of the tyres can permit rapid breaking or otherwise. Apart from the skill and alertness of the driver, the all important factor is the coefficient of friction between the tyres and the road surface. This can be found under simulated road conditions or in the laboratory, such as the Road Research Establishment at Crowthorne. A similar car has to be used in both cases.

Normally the coefficient of friction between tyres and the road varies between 0.7 and 0.8. Because acceleration/deceleration can be defined in terms of friction, then velocity calculations can be carried out. The vital connection, based on Newton's second law of motion, is that $a = \pm$ the coefficient of friction in those circumstances (μ) multiplied by the gravity constant (g). The + and the − are acceleration and deceleration respectively.

If the friction derivation and $v^2 = u^2 + 2as$ are combined, then u, the initial speed, is

$$u = \sqrt{(2\mu gs)} \qquad [v = 0 \text{ because the vehicle comes to rest}]$$

A simple example shows how the calculation is done. The facts are that a car involved in an accident with a pedestrian came to a halt 80 ft after the point of impact. The incident occurred in a 30 mph speed limit zone.

An independent measurement of the stopping distance of a similar vehicle under similar conditions came to 50 ft at 30 mph. The car was obviously speeding but by how much? Conversion to the metric system is simple on the basis of 1 mile = 1.61 km and 1 ft = 0.31 metres.

13

First find the coefficient of friction for the particular circumstances. Refer to the test car.
The co-efficient of friction is

$$\frac{30^2}{2g \times 50} \quad \text{(because } \mu = u^2/2gs\text{)}$$

Now go to the offending car. It came to a halt on the same surface in 80 ft. Its initial velocity u is

$$\sqrt{\left(2 \times \frac{30^2}{2g \times 50} \times g \times 80\right)} \quad \text{[again because } u = \sqrt{(2\mu gs)}\text{]}$$

$$= 38 \text{ mph}$$

To establish the facts of a particular incident, the forensic scientist sometimes goes to the actual accident location and sets up a series of tests with a similar vehicle. This can often cause traffic dislocation.

Realistically, accidents involving moving vehicles cannot be eliminated. Driving with care and in full control of one's reflexes should be the responsibility of all those at the wheel. The young person fresh from a successful driving test passes to a more experienced state when he or she realises that the time available to make a decision in the accident situation is very small. One driving instructor maintained that

"Every other driver on the road is a fool."

It is salutory to realise that other drivers regard oneself in the same light — all too often with justification!

A Last Warning — with 100 mg% blood alcohol level, a person is seven times more likely to be involved in an accident than a person with zero blood alcohol.

2 Drugs

> Heroin is a drug because it affects behaviour but becomes a poison when it kills.

It is difficult to distinguish exactly between a drug and a poison. A drug is a chemical substance that affects psychological or behavioural functions and can lead to varying degrees of dependence or addiction. Scientists often refer to drugs as xenobiotics, which literally means 'foreign to life'. A poison is any chemical substance that can destroy life by its own inherent properties without acting mechanically.

Some drugs have a beneficial effect on the human body, such as the relief of pain, but generally they are not available for energy production or tissue formation. Most people do not include alcohol (ethanol) in their understanding of a drug, despite the fact that it is a powerful depressant of the nervous system. A biochemist could justifiably ask "What right has a middle aged gentleman, retiring to bed on a couple of large brandies and a sleeping tablet, to be critical of a young person smoking 'pot'?" The simple answer is that the law, as it now stands, regards smoking 'pot' as an offence.

Over the past decade or so the news media have made efforts to enlighten the public about the nature of addictive drugs and their effects. Terms such as 'main lining', 'chasing the dragon', 'glue sniffing', 'hard and soft drug' and 'cold turkey' no longer leave the majority perplexed. Of the illegal drugs heroin (derived from the morphine of the opium poppy), cocaine and cannabis are now flooding the Western world. According to one report from the USA, smoking marijuana is more harmful to the lungs than tobacco. The medically prescribed drugs — tranquillisers, antidepressants, sedatives (sleeping pills), amphetamines (pep pills) and the analgesics (pain killers) — are used extensively. In many households there are enough tablets to constitute a risk to health and, in some instances, sufficient for successful suicide or accidental death. What were once considered harmless substances such as solvents, have turned out to be lethal when misused.

15

The parents of a teenage daughter, known to the author, happily retired to bed one evening. The daughter remained on the sofa, alone, watching television. A short while later she started to sniff a 'volatile solvent'. Eventually she collapsed and fell back on to the sofa, unconscious. Her tongue relaxed and retracted into her throat. She died. Next morning her parents found her.

SOME GENERAL FACTS

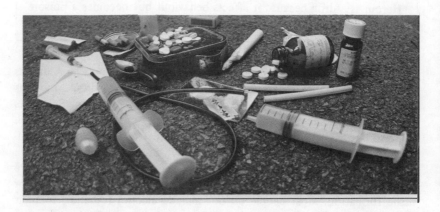

Figure 2.1 *The 'goods' and the 'gear'.*
The missing ingredient is the all-important 'readies' used to finance the 'habit'.

Drugs are, in the main, a medical problem. In cases of abuse, overdose or withdrawal the medical services or their social ancillaries, usually have to pick up the pieces. Whether inhaled, injected or taken by mouth, drugs are distributed around the body in the blood stream. The organ responsible for dealing with foreign substances is the liver, and it is placed under strain when drugs are continually taken. The liver tries to render the drug harmless by changing its chemical structure. It converts drugs to more water-soluble forms for passage to the kidney and elimination in the urine. The rate at which a drug is cleared from the body depends upon its elimination half life. This is the time taken to eliminate 50 per cent of the drug from the body. In the case of all drugs, but especially those medically prescribed, the effective dose is the one that brings about the desired effect. Side effects, which are usually unpleasant, result from the normal intake and often appear unconnected with the desired effect. In some instances, side effects have been more serious than the condition for which the drug was taken. A toxic dose — an intake in excess of the effective dose — gives rise to toxic effects, which are frequently the normal effects exaggerated to the point of discomfort, disturbance or even death. A lethal dose is, as the name suggests, final.

People vary in their reaction to drugs. Tolerance, or the capacity to take a drug without apparent effects, depends on the person and his or her drug habits. In general, frequent intake of a drug is likely to lead to some tolerance. Addiction is indicated if a person suffers withdrawal symptoms when the drug is not taken. It is a useful rule never to take two or more different drugs at the same time. The consequences can be uncomfortable or even fatal.

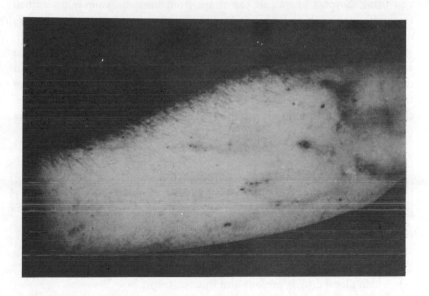

Figure 2.2 *Tell-tale puncture marks.*
The photograph shows marks made by a needle after injection of a drug — probably a drug of abuse.
The danger with self-injection is septicaemia — blood poisoning due to invading bacteria. This happens because personal hygiene usually suffers when drugs are taken. Washing and shaving tend to be forgotten in the 'highs' and 'lows'. Exchanging needles adds the hazards of AIDS and Hepatitis B. Because of these risks, particularly that of AIDS, many drug takers are trying 'snorting' or 'chasing the Dragon' where the drug is inhaled as a powder or as fumes.

THE FORENSIC SCIENTIST'S ROLE

There are two aspects of forensic work related to drugs. Firstly there is direct involvement. If a solid substance is siezed by the police at a 'pop' gathering or by the Customs at a port, then rapid identification and analysis might be required. Does the substance contain an illegal drug or one of its harmful derivatives? When serious road accidents occur and the presence of alcohol (ethanol) is not a factor, then analysis of the body fluids is frequently carried out. This is to establish, or rule out, the presence of a drug or combination of drugs that could cause defective reflex actions. The fluids taken for analysis are blood and urine.

Suspicious death, be it suicide, murder or accident, might have to be investigated for a drug factor. Samples can come from the stomach, various body tissues or the vitreous humour of the eye in addition to the blood and urine. Suspect chemicals can range from substances never prescribed for bodily use, such as Paraquat (a weedkiller) to products with extensive medical use, such as insulin.

Secondly there is indirect involvement. Simply because drugs are illegal and there are those who wish to take them, market forces dictate that money and crime soon become a factor. Around the individual drug user there is constant temptation to finance the 'habit' by theft and petty crime. Blackmail remains an ever present threat. One stipendary Magistrate observed

"Over ninety per cent of the people that appear before me are on drugs. You can tell by the look in their eyes."

When illegal drugs are involved in legal proceedings the Court will want to know:

(a) which illegal drug is present and in what form;
(b) as far as possible, how much of the drug is present; and
(c) what other substances accompany the drug.

THE FIRST STEPS

In order to decide whether an illegal drug is present in a suspicious solid, the scientist can carry out solubility tests (usually the common drugs are not water soluble), pH tests (most drugs are basic or neutral) and spot or colour tests that require specialised chemicals for their action. Specific colour tests are available for cannabis, LSD, amphetamines and cocaine. At the moment there is no reliable colour test for morphine and its heroin derivatives. Microscopic examination of the debris (powder or granules) present in a mix can establish the presence of natural plant structures (leaf fragments) from which cocaine or cannabis might have come. This is additional evidence. Also information can occasionally be gleaned about the geographical origin of the drug — if drug it is. Portions of insects, peculiar to a location, can suggest a particular growing region. The examining forensic scientist must be alert and blessed with a slice or two of luck. Experience is all important. Sometimes the innocent public can be involved in the hunt for illegal drugs.

Recently a friend of the author's took his family off to the South of France for a holiday. The weather was excellent and the wine was good. Quite suddenly his car broke down and he was obliged to leave it at a garage for two days. He had an uneasy feeling that it had been tampered with in some way because he has always been a keen DIY car man. He was given a replacement vehicle while his car was being repaired and the holiday went smoothly.

Leaving the ferry at a Channel port he was surprised to be confronted by a Customs man who waved him aside. He was asked to wait with his family "while certain formalities are attended to." No other vehicle on the entire ferry was treated in this way. Two hours later he was back on the road with a car that had obviously been 'gone over with a fine toothpick".

Throughout he was treated politely and told only that they were on the lookout for drugs.

THE SOPHISTICATED STAGE

After the spot tests, more elaborate procedures are employed to detect, identify and estimate a particular drug. There are two techniques available to the forensic scientist that complement each other — chromatography (already mentioned in chapter 1) and immunoassays. Gas chromatography (GC) and high pressure liquid chromatography (HPLC) require that the sample mixture for analysis is pure — or as free from normal body substances as possible. Accordingly, extraction of the drug(s) from the background material must first be attempted. Thin layer chromatography (TLC)

19

does not need such pure starting mixtures; it can separate the target compounds from the rest, although solvent extraction is often the first step.

SEPARATING OUT THE DRUG

Extraction can involve one or all of the following processes:

(a) the use of selected organic solvents to isolate soluble fractions from insoluble ones;
(b) the employment of two immiscible solvents in contact to separate fractions of relatively different solubilities;
(c) the application of evaporation to discard the volatile portions, such as excess solvent that could complicate the analytical procedures.

An important aspect of extraction is the time factor. Extraction needs to be efficient to deliver the final product in as clean a form as possible. If this takes up too much time, then an adequately clean product prepared in less time might be an advantage.

CHROMATOGRAPHY

In essence any chromatographic procedure separates physically the parts, or components, of a mixture by exploiting the different distributions, or partitions, of each component between two phases. One phase is stationary; the other is mobile and immiscible with the stationary. The components of the mixture must not react with either phase; it is an entirely physical process. The mobile phase is either a gas or a liquid and the stationary phase can be a solid or a liquid adsorbed on, or stuck on to, a solid background. The skill of setting up any chromatographic process is the choice of phases, particularly the stationary phase.

THIN LAYER CHROMATOGRAPHY

Thin layer chromatography (TLC) is used extensively both medically and forensically in the screening for drugs. Screening is the recognition of the actual presence, or absence, of a particular drug in a large number of individual samples. Estimation of precise quantities present is then carried out by GC or HPLC.

Most people know that if a spot of ink is placed on some dry blotting or filter paper and the end placed in water, the water creeps up the paper taking the ink with it. The water naturally travels faster than the ink. If the ink is made up of a mixture of coloured pigments, the colours are separated as they move up the paper. This is basically paper chromatography. The stationary phase is the fibres of the paper to which some water is adsorbed. The mobile phase is the water which is immiscible with the paper and is dragged up it by capillary attraction. In all chromatography there must be some means of pushing, or dragging, the mobile phase along. The separation of the colours is brought about by the different distributions, or partitions, of the various pigments between the paper and the mobile water. Some pigments stick to the paper more than others, which might be less soluble in the water. Those that are not readily adsorbed to the paper are taken up farther.

Thin layer chromatography works on the same principle. The stationary phase is a thin layer of a chemical such as silica, and the mobile phase is the solvent chosen for the occasion. It is important that all the target components to be separated should be, to some extent, soluble in the mobile phase. As with the paper, the silica slows down certain components more than others. Separation is thereby effected and the process can be stopped by removing the thin layer plate from the solvent. The thin layer can then be dried and sprayed with a suitable stain or illuminated with ultra-violet light. In this way the individual spots become visible and their positions apparent.

The distance a component travels up the background layer relative to the distance travelled by the solvent front is known as the R_f value. Thus

$$R_f = \frac{\text{distance travelled by the component}}{\text{distance travelled by the solvent (mobile phase)}}$$

The R_f value of any compound relates to its behaviour on a thin layer or paper using a particular solvent. If the same mixture of drugs or dyes is subjected to TLC using several different solvents, then the R_f value of a certain compound will be different for each solvent. This gives a method of cross-checking for a target compound.

GAS CHROMATOGRAPHY

With GC the stationary phase is frequently a liquid which is locked on to a solid background to prevent it moving. Sometimes it is a solid on its own. The mobile phase is an inert gas that is immiscible with the stationary phase on the separation unit, or column. This gas, introduced under pressure,

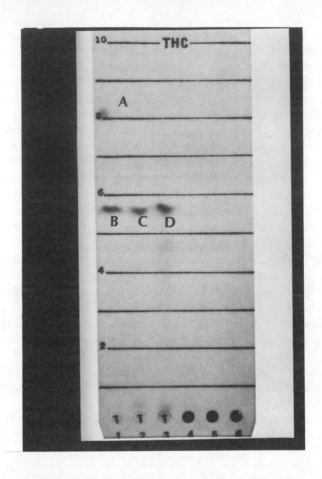

Figure 2.3 *Spotting a drug*

A substance, removed from a person in suspicious circumstances, is suspected to be an illegal drug. A quick method to find out is thin layer chromatography.

The photograph shows the distribution of spots after the 'run' and appropriate staining. The suspected drug is actually cannabis.

T is the point of application of three samples; lane 1 is standard cannabis as a control; lane 2 is the unknown; lane 3 is a standard derivative of cannabis. A is the level reached by the solvent when the 'run' was stopped (merely by removing the thin layer from the solvent). B, C and D are the spots that appeared in the three lanes when stain was applied.

Since the R_f values of all three are the same then, subject to further confirmation, the unknown substance contains cannabis or its derivative.

carries the component mixture into the column and along the stationary phase. One point about GC is that the components of the injected mixture must be volatile in order to be separated. It is obvious how impurities can mess things up. The situation is maybe similar to a carburettor with the wayward fragment of dirt.

Control of conditions, such as temperature and type of stationary phase, influence the efficiency of separation. This again is due to the partitioning of the various components between the liquid or solid and the gas mobile phase.

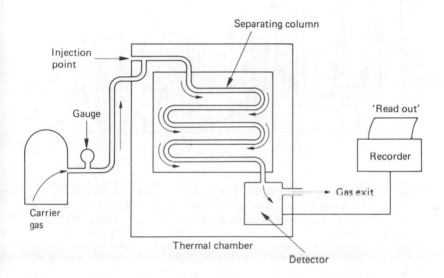

Figure 2.4 *A simple flow diagram of a GC system.*

In a way, progress of a mixture through a GC system or column is like a race between sailing craft on water. All start at the same time (injection time) and progress of individuals is influenced by the action of the wind (mobile phase) on the craft and by the retarding action of the water (stationary phase). In the end the race is won by the craft first past the post (the first to elute from the column) and so on down to the last to finish. The time taken from the start to the finish for any craft (from injection to elution) is known as the 'retention time'. Each component has its own characteristic retention time (similar to the R_f value in TLC) and this is shown as a distance along one axis of the 'read out'.

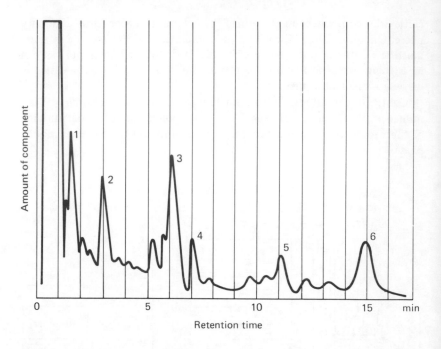

Figure 2.5 *Gasoline on a graph.*
A gas chromatograph 'read out' of Two Star Texaco Ordinary petrol. The components have been separated from the mixture according to the time (retention time) at which each emerges from the separating column.
The peaks represent: 1 benzene; 2 toluene; 3 m-xylene; 4 xylene; 5 butyl benzene; 6 trimethyl benzene.
Peaks 3 and 4, although close together, are distinctly separate. This is a reflection of the resolution of the separating process. If close peaks are clear and can be distinguished easily from each other, the resolution is good.

HIGH PRESSURE LIQUID CHROMATOGRAPHY

HPLC has as its stationary phase a column of finely divided solid packing material (typically each unit being 10 μm in size). A liquid is the mobile phase and this is forced through the separating column under pressure. Relative partitioning of the components between the liquid and the solid effects the separation. After detection of the eluting compounds there is the usual 'read out', which often takes some experience (and imagination) to interpret. With HPLC the components of the mixture must be soluble in the mobile phase.

24

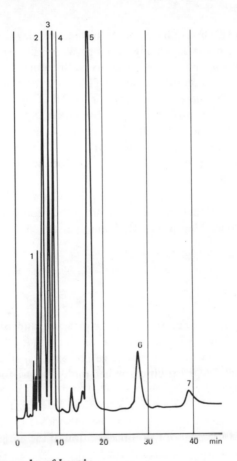

Figure 2.6 The peaks of heroin.
The end result of passing a sample of commercial heroin through an HPLC column.

Along the horizontal, or x, axis is the time taken for a component to pass through the separating column. This time is the retention time and is referred to as t_r. For any set of separating conditions, a particular component has a definite retention time.

The y, or vertical, axis represents the amount of component emerging at a particular retention time.

On the graph shown: 1 is barbitol; 2 is caffeine; 3 is acetyl codeine; 4 is heroin; 5 is monoacetylmorphine; 6 is strychnine; 7 is morphine.

If an unknown mixture suspected of containing heroin is passed through the column, the retention times of the emerging components indicate the identity of the compounds present. Known specimens of heroin etc. (controls) have to be run at the same time as a check.

SFC (Supercritical Fluid Chromatography) is halfway between GC and HPLC. The mobile phase is a gas (CO_2 or NH_3) just above its critical point. This allows more efficient diffusion and separation.

Both GC and HPLC require detector systems to pick out the components emerging from the separating column. With TLC, sprays that stain selectively reveal the spots of drugs or dyes. Sometimes ultra-violet light or a laser beam is used on the spots on a TLC plate to show their positions by fluorescence. The detector system for the HPLC is usually a spectrophotometer and that for the GC a Flame Ionisation Detector (FID).

TLC is more flexible than either GC or HPLC. It is relatively easy to perform and requires fewer resources (HPLC is often referred to as 'high priced liquid chromatography'). However, TLC does not yield such accurate or quantifiable results as GC or HPLC.

In a court of law, chromatographic evidence needs, if possible, to be backed up by confirmatory results from other sources. Based on an entirely different working principle, immunoassays are excellent for this purpose.

IMMUNOASSAYS

An immunoassay is designed to detect the presence, and estimate the concentration, of a target substance using the techniques of immunology. Immunoassays rely on the fact that large proteins, called antibodies, can recognise and lock on to specific smaller molecules to form a complex. These specific smaller molecules are called antigens. The antibodies lock on to definite sites on the surface known as determinants or epitopes. Using appropriate labelling techniques, the antibody/antigen complex can give a precise measurement of the concentration of the antigen. If the antigen happens to be a drug, the advantages from the forensic and the medical point of view are obvious. An antibody can 'pluck out' an antigen (maybe a drug) from background material that might be in urine or blood plasma. Thus immunoassays can be used as screening, as well as precise measuring, systems.

> "An antibody can be produced against anything".

Such was the optimistic claim of one biochemist working in the field of immunoassay techniques. If an antigen, such as cocaine, is injected into an animal, such as a sheep, goat or rabbit, the animal will obligingly produce antibodies against that antigen − usually without harm to itself. If the molecules of the antigen are too small to stimulate the immune response, they have to be modified in some way before being injected to produce the antibodies. This modification process, called derivatisation, represents a challenge to the able biochemist. Any change to the antigen must not interfere with its epitope or binding site.

After producing the antibodies the animal is bled, usually from the ear, and the serum is separated out of the blood. Using the original antigen as a detector, the serum is screened and the required antibodies are extracted and stored for use in an immunoassay.

The first step is to mix a known amount of the antibody ⟨⟩ with a known excess of antigen molecules ○ . These antigen molecules are labelled in some way so that their progress can be monitored.

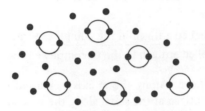

The antibodies bind on to the antigen to form complexes, but there are spare labelled antigen molecules left over — about 50 per cent. Into this mix is now added a solution (urine) containing an unknown amount of antigen, whose molecules are not labelled. The aim is to find out how much unlabelled antigen there is in the urine (the antigen could be a target drug such as cannabis). The unlabelled antigen molecules are represented by ● .

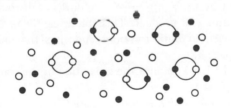

When the unlabelled antigen molecules enter the situation there is competition for the antigen binding sites on the surface of the antibodies. The newly arrived unlabelled molecules displace the labelled ones. As would be expected from an orderly Nature, this displacement is in direct proportion to the concentration of unlabelled antigen added. So, after an incubation period to establish an equilibrium, the mix is centrifuged, or subjected to a separation process. This results in two fractions: one containing all the antibodies that are complexed to either labelled or unlabelled antigen, the

27

other containing all other molecules. The amount of labelled antigen in both fractions can be estimated. The smaller the labelling response from the antibody complex fraction, the more unlabelled antigen added in the urine.

This does not give precise information about the concentration of the unlabelled antigen. Such information can only be acquired after the construction of a standard curve. Unknowns can then be assessed by reference to this curve.

Constructing a standard curve involves carrying out the assay procedure just described with a series of known concentrations of unlabelled antigen. For each sample of the series a ratio is calculated:

$$\frac{\text{labelled antigen in the complexed fraction}}{\text{labelled antigen in the uncomplexed fraction}}$$

A graph is then drawn. Along the x axis is plotted the series of known concentrations of antigen at the start; along the y axis is the corresponding ratio of labelled complexed/uncomplexed at the end. Future unknown concentrations can be found from this curve.

There are three methods of labelling available at present.

(a) *Radio Immune Assay (RIA)*
Attached to the antigen is a molecule or group that contains a radioactive element such as ^{125}I.

(b) *Enzyme Linked Immunosorbent Assay (ELISA)*
The antigen is labelled by an attached enzyme. The activity of the enzyme can be estimated by the addition of a colourless substrate, which is converted to a coloured end product. This colour can be quantified revealing the labelled antigen in both fractions and thus the unlabelled antigen added (see also page 37).

Both RIA and ELISA require the separation of the complexed fraction from the uncomplexed.

(c) *Fluorescence Polarisation Immune Assay (FPIA)*
The antigen molecules are labelled with fluorescein and the equilibrium mixture is subjected to polarised light. The emerging light signal depends on the number of labelled antigen molecules complexed with the antibodies. A high final signal means a low initial addition of unlabelled antigen and vice versa.

A standard curve is necessary with FPIA but this can be plotted regularly and stored in the memory of the electronic section of the machine. FPIA does not require the separation of the complexed from the uncomplexed fractions. For this reason it could be the immune assay of the future.

One authority has stated that the FPIA can detect cannabis in the urine of a person who smoked one single 'joint' two weeks previously. Precise estimation can go to the femtomolar level $(10^{-15}$ M).

At the present time, RIA and ELISA are in regular use in forensic laboratories.

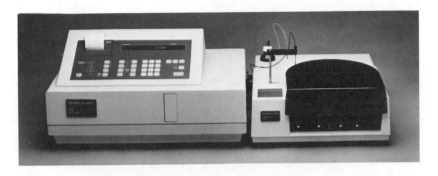

Figure 2.7 *Rapid, highly sensitive, drug screening (courtesy of Perkin-Elmer) (see also table 2.1).*

The photograph shows the latest in drug screening – an automated machine for carrying out Fluorescence Polarisation Immune Assays (FPIA) now in use in some hospitals. For promotion purposes, an appropriate environment has been chosen.

The specimens for screening (urine, for example) are placed in the compartment on the right. A rotating platform, or carousel, brings each specimen in turn to the sampler. This transfers a given amount into the left compartment – a spectrometer – for measurement.

It is perhaps worth a mention that most modern automated laboratory equipment (so-called 'black boxes') look more or less the same – compact and deceptively simple. This is because the electronic control of processes and the handling of data has revolutionised instrument design. In the past, before the advent of the 'chip', machines that were complicated actually looked complicated.

Large molecules, such as proteins, have complex and individual surfaces. Each molecule of a particular protein has a unique and common surface topography with its own charge (positive or negative) distribution. Surface binding sites on antibodies, to which antigens link, are highly specific.

Specificity means that a method of investigation shows a clear response to a single type of target compound. Background material, normally present in urine or blood plasma, does not affect the ability of antibodies to 'pluck out' the relevant molecules for quantitative assessment. Good specificity implies an efficient quantitative use; high sensitivity implies an efficient quantitative estimation.

```
FILE  3 MORPHINE
SCREENING TEST
CONTROL CONC.: 1.00 mg/L
READY FOR SAMPLES

A/C SEQU. FOR 40 SAMPLES

SAMPLES RUN ON ........

    ID  DISPLAY  CONC
    1QC  89.4  CONTROL
    2    71.5  POS.
    3    63.8  POS.
    4   121.5  NEG.
    5   117.3  NEG.
    6   120.7  NEG.
    7   115.8  NEG.
    8   116.0  NEG.
    9    66.9  POS.
   10   114.7  NEG.
   11   115.5  NEG.
   12    86.0  POS.
   13    68.0  POS.
   14   109.0  NEG.
   15    56.6  POS.
   16    99.2  NEG.
   17    71.1  POS.
   18    66.4  POS.
   19    74.8  POS.
   20    93.5  NEG.
   21    81.2  POS.
   22    71.1  POS.
   23   103.3  NEG.
   24   121.6  NEG.
   25   134.3  NEG.
   26    68.5  POS.
   27   110.0  NEG.
   28    74.1  POS.
   29   121.2  NEG.
   30    67.0  POS.
   31    85.1  POS.
   32    95.8  NEG.
   33    66.6  POS.
   34    74.4  POS.
   35    67.6  POS.
   36    50.0  POS.
   37    85.3  POS.
   38    66.0  POS.
   39    66.1  POS.
   40    72.9  POS.
A/C SEQUENCE TERMINATED
```

Table 2.1 *Rapid, highly sensitive, drug screening (courtesy of Perkin-Elmer) (see also figure 2.7).*

A record of 40 samples screened for morphine in the apparatus illustrated in figure 2.7 is shown.

Normally in an immune assay, the higher the output number in the 'print out' the more the target molecules (in this case morphine) present. With FPIA the reverse is true: the higher the signal, or output number, the lower the level of unlabelled target molecules. In this 'run', when a display number exceeds the control figure of 89.4, a negative result is recorded.

The concentration of morphine in that sample is below the control level.

WIDER CONSIDERATIONS

Drug trafficking is big business. The demand for illegal drugs is on the increase and maintaining the supply needs careful planning and detailed organisation. Heroin has to be extracted from the opium poppy, purified and distributed through an international network of 'contacts'. Cocaine has to be obtained from the leaves of the coca plant and then transported for many miles before reaching 'the street'. Additives, themselves harmful, are frequently mixed with the pure drug to increase profits. Many people are involved in the transporting and marketing of illegal drugs and anyone who 'steps out of line' pays heavily.

The need for an illegal drug is created first by the pedlars who 'push' the drug — sometimes to twelve year old children. Because the drugs are addictive, this need becomes a craving. Those who become 'hooked' will do anything to satisfy this craving and the bosses of the international drug rings amass vast fortunes. These gentlemen are very powerful and utterly ruthless. In the words of one officer of the law: "These boys make up the rules as they go along — bribery, corruption, murder, arson, anything goes."

A person who takes illegal drugs is constantly open to blackmail. If that person is entrusted with classified information, then pressure can be exerted by agents of a hostile government. Silence is bought by passing state secrets.

Human ingenuity is shown at its best — or maybe at its worst — by those who smuggle illegal drugs.

One audacious character developed the trick of swallowing heroin tied up inside condoms. The drugs stayed in his stomach and were recovered at the appropriate time by vomiting. Success and handsome dividends made him careless and he swallowed too many filled condoms all at once. Some ruptured in his stomach and others blocked his gut. Before he could reach his destination he died in agony.

Most people have heard of the existence of suitcases with cunningly concealed compartments, of women's shoes with hollow heels and of waterproof packages hidden in petrol tanks. Most of these stratagems must be successful because only a small percentage of the illegal drugs that enter the UK are seized by Customs. Many of the Customs' spectacular hauls result from a tip off. A number of sincere people believe that legalising the use of certain 'soft' drugs would reduce the involvement of big time criminals in the drug business. Cannabis is the example most frequently cited to back up this conviction.

Recent figures show that approximately the same number of people (100) die each year in the UK from

(a) injuries sustained on a sports field;
(b) the abuse of volatile substances (glue sniffing, etc.);
(c) the use of hard drugs. (In this case the number is derived from those removed from the official register — presumably because of death.)

3 Trace Evidence – the Body Fluids

Trace evidence is invariably small in quantity and scanty in distribution. Frequently it is difficult to detect. It consists, principally, of fluids (usually in the form of stains) and discrete particles or fibres that a criminal leaves at, or takes from, the scene of a crime. Also marks — some of them very faint — are often left to indicate 'suspicious circumstances'. One Founding Father of forensic science firmly maintained that

> "every contact leaves a trace" — a sobering thought!

Fluids from the human body that may constitute trace evidence are one, several or all of blood, sweat, saliva, urine, tears, semen and vaginal secretions. In many cases the fluid will have been exposed to the elements before forensic examination. Drying or decay and deterioration inevitably result from exposure. Often the constituents of body fluids are changed by the substratum on which they are deposited.

Analysis and investigation of body fluids is the task of the forensic biochemist, who would perhaps amend the Biblical statement to

> "By their body fluids ye shall know them".

Biochemistry has rightly been described as "probing into the unseen." Processes that go on at the molecular level — shifts across electric fields, migration through gels, union of one active site with another, cutting or splicing of polymer chains — are silent and not directly observable. Such phenomena can only be detected by, or inferred from, peaks on a graph 'read out', numbers on a counter or dial, and coloured or fluorescent bands. Interpretation of the actual observations and their relevance, or relationship, to molecular behaviour requires the use of reason, intelligent guesswork and imagination in varying proportions.

THE MAJOR BODY FLUID – BLOOD

According to the circumstances of a case, it may be necessary to show the presence of a particular body fluid on a garment or object. The most common body fluid left, or taken, as trace evidence is blood. A few drops probably contain more information about the person from which it came than most of the other body fluids taken together. In blood there are many genetic markers (blood groups) that can characterise the individual from which it came. However a red smear may not be blood, so an initial test is necessary to establish the presence of blood.

This test uses the peroxidase-like activity of haemoglobin, a constituent of all blood samples of forensic interest. If hydrogen peroxide and a suitable indicator (o-tolidine or reduced phenolphthalein) is added to the blood extract, the peroxidase-like activity of the haemoglobin liberates oxygen. This oxidises the indicator to a distinctive colour – in the case of phenolphthalein it is pink.

> This test is a presumptive test in that a positive result means that it probably is blood but it is not certain. The test works with plant peroxidases but not rust.

The next step is to find the species from which the blood came. A positive result to this establishes the presence of blood with certainty. The basis of the species test is the antibody–antigen fusion reaction. All blood contains certain molecules called antigens. Some of these antigens are located on the surface of red corpuscles. If these antigens are exposed to their complementary antibodies, complexes are formed. When antibodies lock on to antigens on the surface of red cells, the cells (corpuscles) clump together, or agglutinate. A supply of appropriate antibodies is a major requirement for the species test. If human blood is injected into an animal (sheep or goat) the animal responds by producing antibodies against the foreign antigens. These anti-human antibodies can be isolated from the animal.

A drop of liquid containing the anti-human antibodies is placed in a small well made in the centre of a thin square of Agar jelly. Around this central well is a circle of six or eight wells of similar size. Into each outer well, except one, is placed a specimen of blood of known origin such as human, dog, cat, etc. These are the controls. The last well contains the blood of unknown origin. Antibody and antigen molecules diffuse through the gel in all directions. In between the wells they meet. If antibodies from the central well meet antigens from human blood then complexes will form. According to viewing conditions, these complexes show up as dark bands on a light background or light bands on a dark background. Antigens from non-human blood will not form complexes with the antibodies raised against human blood.

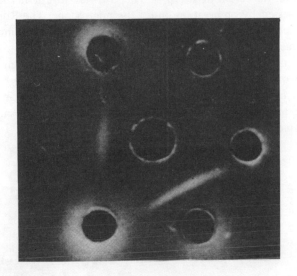

Figure 3.1 *Species identification of blood (copyright American Society for Testing and Materials – reproduced with permission).*
In the centre well is placed antibodies against human blood.
A definite light band is formed in the Agar between the central well and the outer well containing known human blood. A fainter light band occurs between the central well and that containing the unknown sample. This indicates the presence of human blood in the unknown.
The controls in the other outer wells – dog's blood, sheep's blood, etc. – do not react with the antibodies in the central well.

The process of diffusion is, by itself, quite slow so in practice it is often speeded up by placing the Agar jelly (known as the gel) in an electric field.

THE AB0 BLOOD GROUPS

Grouping, or typing, of blood for transfusion purposes has long been practised in hospitals. The blood of the donor must have the same grouping as that of the recipient. They must match. The best known blood groups are the ABO and Rhesus systems. All blood groups are genetically determined.

When blood of group A is mixed with blood of group B then the red corpuscles clump together, or agglutinate. The antigens on the surface of the red cells (corpuscles) of group A are recognised as 'foreign' by the antibodies in the serum of group B. The two fuse together. The clumping can be assessed by observation under the microscope. The Rhesus factor can be detected in the same way — Rhesus positive blood is incompatible with Rhesus negative blood.

This type of blood grouping is reliable and accurate if there are ample quantities of fresh blood available, as would be the case in a hospital. At the scene of a crime there is frequently insufficient raw material left around. Sometimes the ABO test has to be omitted in favour of more sophisticated tests.

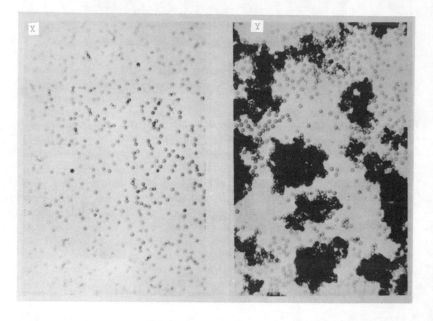

Figure 3.2 *Testing for the ABO blood groups (see also table 3.1).*
The old routine. On the left (X) is blood of group A. To this has been added serum from blood of the same group. The red corpuscles remain as normal. On the right (Y), serum from blood of group B has been added to the group A blood. The red corpuscles clump together, or agglutinate. This process can actually be seen and assessed under the microscope.

	(NO SALIVA)(CELIA)	(HELEN)	(SELF)	(HELEN G.)	(DALE)	(NAN)	(CJC)	(OIA)	(JANE)	(AJS)	(MARK)
	1	2	3 M	4	5	6	7	8	9	10	11	12
A	-.000	-.002	-.003	-.005	-.006	-.005	-.003	-.004	0.001	0.007	0.009	0.023
B	-.006	-.001	-.008	-.006	-.011	-.002	-.008	-.003	0.003	0.005	0.009	0.011
C	-.005	0.008	0.262	-.000	0.341	0.008	-.003	-.001	-.001	0.161	-.003	0.302
D	0.002	0.011	0.342	0.003	0.280	0.006	-.008	-.000	0.001	0.160	0.001	0.232
E	0.012	0.007	0.272	0.010	0.276	0.016	-.009	0.009	-.004	0.188	0.013	0.282
F	-.001	0.001	0.004	0.019	0.004	0.015	0.346	0.272	-.003	0.022	0.118	0.015
G	-.005	0.008	0.001	0.014	-.001	0.011	0.400	0.445	-.000	0.017	0.111	0.013
H	0.050	-.002	0.010	-.008	0.008	0.005	0.614	0.639	0.003	0.004	0.195	0.011

A&B- Control   C, D, E - ANTI-A   F, G, H - ANTI-B.

Table 3.1 *Testing for the AB0 blood groups (see also figure 3.2). The 'print out' — the new system.*

Data from an actual immuno assay (ELISA) designed to find the AB0 grouping of saliva from eleven individuals. Specially sensitive antibodies, called monoclonal antibodies, are added to the saliva samples. These antibodies bind to any AB0 antigens present in the saliva. The degree of binding is indicated by a colour reaction which is assessed and recorded as a number. The bigger the number, the greater the depth of colour and the higher the concentration of antigen in the saliva.

Column 1 has no saliva and is a control — so no colour.

Rows A and B have no antibodies added and are also controls. Rows C, D and E have antibodies against the antigen of blood group A; rows F, G and H have antibodies against the antigen of blood group B. The numbers in column 2 (Celia) show that there are no group A or B antigens present. Celia has no AB0 antigens in her saliva, or indeed her other body fluids. She is a non-secretor, a status that is conferred genetically, and inherited from her parents.

In column 3 (Helen M), high numbers are found in rows C, D and E. Helen is thus of blood group A and secretes these antigens into her saliva and other body fluids.

The high numbers in rows F, G and H in column 7 (Nan) indicate a secretor of the blood group B antigen.

Testing for the AB0 groups in body fluids can be useful when investigating cases of rape.

The victim (a young woman) was subjected to rape by five men. Her cries attracted a passing police car and all six were taken in. The table shows the results of AB0 grouping of the seminal fluids found on the victim and the suspects. The swab was a vaginal swab. The blood group of the person is shown in column two and the victim is a non-secretor of the AB0 antigens into her body fluids.

37

Table 3.2 A case of multiple rape

Individual and own groups		Seminal groups found	
Victim	A non-secretor	Skirt	A secretor
			Non-secretor
		Swab	A secretor
		Pants	AB secretor
Suspect 1	0 secretor	Pants	A secretor
		Shirt	0 secretor
Suspect 2	0 secretor	Trousers	A secretor
Suspect 3	A secretor	Pants	AB secretor
Suspect 4	AB secretor	Pants	AB secretor
Suspect 5	Non-secretor	Pants	A secretor
		Penis	0 secretor

On the basis of this grouping it was suggested that the rapes were carried out in the following order – suspect 4 first, suspect 3 second, suspect 2 next, then suspect 5 and lastly suspect 1.

THE GENETIC MARKERS

There are many genetic markers in the blood that do not rely on red cell clumping for their recognition. Many of these markers are enzymes – PGM or phosphoglucomutase, for example – and a different technique is used to detect them.

All body fluids contain proteins that are produced in response to instructions from the DNA in the genes. With the exception of identical twins all individuals are genetically unique. Exploration of the body fluids can thus give good indications of the genetic make up, and perhaps identity, of the donor. The molecules of body proteins often have sugars attached to them and the type of sugar, as well as its manner of attachment, is also genetically controlled. Inherited biochemicals rarely change during life and many can be detected by simple specific tests.

Offspring inherit two genes (one from each parent) responsible for the production of a particular protein. This means that there can be more than one type of that protein, although only one particular type would be found in any individual.

> This is known as Polymorphism and is one source of the variation found in living organisms.

With regard to PGM already mentioned, there are three molecular types (namely 1-1, 2-1 and 2-2) produced by a pair of genes. Everybody has one of these types in his or her blood. Each type of PGM molecule differs slightly from the other two, but all three give positive results to the specific PGM test. The slight differences between the three forms means that the process of electrophoresis can be used to detect each type.

By means of mass screening or testing, the frequency of each PGM type (1-1, 2-1, 2-2) can be found for a population. These frequencies can then be expressed as fractions or percentages of the total. From this data the frequency of the two genes, or alleles, can be calculated. These statistics are of use when comparing two blood samples to decide the probability of obtaining a match between them. How likely is it that the two samples came from the same source?

MATCHING OF BLOOD SAMPLES

If blood from a suspect and blood found at a scene of crime are both of the PGM type 1-1, they obviously match. But over 50 per cent of the general population are of the 1-1 type so the probability of obtaining such a match is high. Consequently the likelihood that the blood from the suspect and the blood from the scene came from the same source is low — despite the fact that they are both of the same type as regards PGM.

If the blood specimens are now examined for another marker that exists in eight or nine forms (as might be the case with the blood protein haptoglobin) and indicates that more than two genes are involved, then fewer people in a population will belong to each type. In this case it is more significant if blood from the suspect matches that from the crime scene. The probability of obtaining a purely random match of two blood samples within this second marker system (haptoglobin) is much lower than for PGM. So, if the blood from the suspect and from a crime scene match, that is they have the same haptoglobin type, then the likelihood that they came from the same source (the suspect) is correspondingly higher. Also if two samples match for two different markers then the chance that the two samples came from the same source increases. With three markers the chance is higher still.

Calculations regarding the matching of blood samples can only be done if the frequency of the different types within each separate grouping system is known for a particular population — see table 3.3.

Calculating the probability that two blood samples — one from the suspect and one from the crime scene — come from the same source must take account of two factors:

(a) the number of molecular types produced by the genes governing each marker;
(b) the number of marker systems tested.

However certainty is not possible. Even the most likely matching might be entirely chance and nothing else.

From a forensic point of view, a genetic marker must have the following characteristics:

(i) There must be several (as many as possible) distinct types.
(ii) These types must remain unchanged throughout life in a readily available body fluid, preferably blood. Many of the markers occur in most body fluids. PGM actually occurs in hair roots.
(iii) There must be an easy, quick and reliable method for detecting each type and discriminating between them.
(iv) All the types of a marker must be capable of withstanding the rigours of the environment. Forensic samples are usually shed at random on varying backgrounds. Analysis may take place days, weeks even, after deposit. One disadvantage of the ABO blood grouping system is that the biochemicals (the antigens on the surface of the red cells) change on exposure to moisture and bacterial action.

When a stain is removed from a crime scene, it is necessary to take as a control another piece of the background or substratum — maybe a piece of clothing — from an area close to the stain removed. This covers the possibility that the stain is an artefact caused by the background itself.

The identification of blood groups, or marker types, by red cell agglutination has its problems. Fresh controls of cells and antibodies are required daily and the inspection of agglutination microscopically relies heavily on the interpretation of the observer. The recent introduction of the ELISA technique (see table 3.1) has improved the situation regarding ABO typing.

40

Table 3.3 Frequencies of three common blood types (as percentage)

System	Type	European (white)	African (black)
AB0	A	40.4	27.5
	B	9.4	19.5
	0	47.4	49.5
	AB	3.2	3.5
Rhesus	Rh positive	83.6	93.6
	Rh negative	16.4	6.4
PGM	1–1	58.8	63.6
	2–1	35.6	31.9
	2–2	5.6	4.5

ELECTROPHORESIS

A reliable method for typing the genetic blood markers — for example, PGM and haptoglobin — is electrophoresis. Large molecules, such as proteins, have small electrical charges distributed over their surfaces. When a mixture of proteins is placed in a gel, or jelly-like medium, and subjected to the forces in an electric field, the protein molecules migrate. Some move towards the anode or positive end; some move towards the cathode or negative end. Smaller molecules move more rapidly than the larger ones. Electrophoresis exploits the different mobilities of molecules such as proteins. It is basically a separation technique. The nature and density of the gel influence the migration, as does the voltage employed.

Different genetically determined forms of the same protein will, under suitable conditions, move at different speeds. After the 'run' these different forms can be identified by suitable staining, or visualisation.

If a small quantity of blood, or blood extract from a blood stain, is placed on a gel, the proteins will migrate in response to the voltage applied. After a certain time each protein will arrive at a point determined by its molecular size and surface charge distribution. From a few microlitres of starting material there could eventually be many proteins spaced along the gel (see figure 3.4).

Detecting a particular target protein is done by using a specific stain or process that shows up one type of molecule in preference to others. This visualisation is based on the natural action and structure of the protein concerned. Apart from colour, fluorescence and radioactivity are used to detect particles on a gel. Recently antibodies have been used for this purpose. This is possible because of the active sites on the surfaces of all

41

proteins. Antibodies form complexes with these active sites and it is the complexes that are visualised. Highly specific antibodies can be produced that 'latch on' to one particular active site. These are called monoclonal antibodies. Sometimes the required proteins are 'blotted', or lifted, off the gel on to special paper before being visualised by staining or antibody fusion. This makes photographic recording easier.

The value of electrophoresis lies in the fact that the types within a genetic marker usually have different mobilities in a given gel under specific conditions.

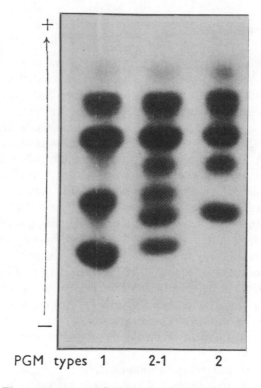

Figure 3.3 *Electrophoresis of PGM – the end result.*
The arrow shows the direction in which the proteins migrate through the gel. The source of the PGM enzyme – usually a small drop of blood or the root of a single hair – is applied at the negative end of the gel.
The staining procedure, to visualise the PGM at the end of the run, makes use of the biochemical activity of the PGM molecules.

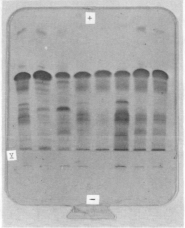

Figure 3.4 *High-tech electrophoresis (courtesy of Pharmacia Ltd).*
The upper photograph shows a fully automated laboratory instrument for separating, and then visualising, the components of a mixture by electrophoresis. Appropriately, it is called the Phastsystem. Specially prepared thin gels, usually of acrylamide, are placed on the areas marked out in the chamber on the left. The time and working conditions of the 'run' are controlled by a computer in the central part. After separation, the components are not visible, so staining has to be carried out. The right-hand compartment is where this is done.
The lower photograph shows a gel — about $1\frac{1}{4}$ times its normal size — on which eight different 0.5 µl samples of blood sera were placed at the origin (X). After electrophoresis for an hour at 550 volts, the gel was stained with Coomassie Blue to show up proteins. The bands, coloured blue, are where the proteins of the blood sera finished at the end of the 'run'.
After staining, the gel can be dried slowly and made into a slide for display on a 35 mm projector. On the far right of the Phastsystem is a screen and slide carrier for magnified observation of completed gels.

A PGM 1-1 gives a different end colour pattern from either the 2-1 or the 2-2 types.

An electrophoretic refinement introduced a short while ago is to create bands of definite pH in the gel itself. Alkaline pH bands at one end of the gel merge into neutral pH bands in the middle with acidic pH bands at the other end. The molecules migrate as usual but then come to rest at a particular pH band in the gel. Further application of the voltage does not move the proteins. This system is called iso electric focusing (IEF). In the case of PGM shown in figure 3.3 more bands show up with IEF. This indicates that there are subtypes within the normal types. Reliable typing of small extracts from old, dried blood stains are possible by this method.

There are, of course, problems with electrophoresis. These include heating effects, the correct buffer to use, the best voltage for separation and the nature and thickness of the gel. Refinements of the present techniques are being developed and marketed almost daily — or so it seems! (See figure 3.4.)

DNA FINGERPRINTING

The most recent advance in exploring genetic markers is to penetrate to the DNA itself. The result has been DNA fingerprinting, successfully developed at the University of Leicester.

DNA extracted from the cells of blood, semen, etc. is digested, or broken up, by restriction enzymes and subsequent alkali treatment into short lengths of single-strand DNA. Normally DNA exists as a double-stranded helix. Only specific and pre-selected portions of the DNA twin strands are digested in this way. The enzymes cut the DNA strands at definite sites. The resulting short strands are separated by electrophoresis in gels and then located with probes. The separated 'bits' are blotted off the gel before the application of the probes. These are short lengths of specially constructed single-stranded DNA. They join up with the target fragments to restore the helical structure. Labelling is effected by incorporating radio-active phosphorus into the probes. Photographic techniques are used to visualise the radioactive fused pairs. The end product is a number of bands showing dark on a light background.

Any individual has his or her own particular arrangement of bands and this reflects the uniqueness of each individual at the genetic or DNA level. Lane 2 in figure 3.5 is a DNA fingerprint of the male's blood and lane 3 is a fingerprint of the female's blood. The vaginal swabs from which the fingerprint in lane 1 was derived, were taken 6 hours after intercourse.

The forensic use of DNA fingerprinting centres on the fact that an individual can be identified exactly — or within a whisker of certainty.

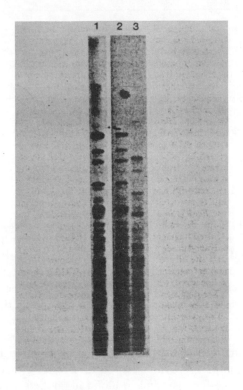

Figure 3.5 *DNA fingerprinting (courtesy of* Nature *journal).*

After the digested DNA portions have been separated on a gel (usually agarose), they are 'blotted off' and then linked to, or hybridised with, the labelled probes.

The blot is placed against an autoradiograph film for several days at minus 70° C in the dark. The result is an autoradiograph, which can be photographed. This is the DNA fingerprint shown in the photograph.

The sperm cells in the vaginal swab (the origin of the bands in lane 1), almost certainly came from the same male as the blood from which lane 2 is derived.

Recent research has been devoted to exploring the possibility of fingerprinting the DNA of horses. Such fingerprints would then be part of the recorded pedigree of the animal. Now that stud fees run into thousands of pounds and artificial insemination is on the increase, particularly in the USA, proof of paternity could be invaluable to breeders. This would be a certain way of checking that a batch of semen came from a particular sire. In addition, fingerprinting could assist in the hunt for a stolen horse of high market value – which these days means millions of pounds or dollars. In some literature 'profiling' is used instead of 'fingerprinting'.

It has been estimated that the probability of obtaining a completely chance match using the DNA fingerprinting technique is 3×10^{-11}. This turns out to be one chance in thirty three billion — which is over six times the present world population.

One minor complication is that identical twins have the same DNA fingerprint.

At the moment, the procedure takes quite a long time and the radio-active phosphorus has a relatively short half life, which make the process expensive. Also probes tend to be jealously guarded by those who develop them.

DNA fingerprinting is used nowadays in cases of paternity and, to a lesser extent, of rape. The DNA fingerprint of any one person shows bands from both parents. Half the bands come from the mother; half from the father. A comparison of the DNA fingerprints of the putative parent and the offspring gives a virtually certain answer to the question — is this man the father of this child? In the case of rape or assault the matching of blood from a suspect and blood removed from the clothes or body of a victim can approach the probability of 1 — which is certainty. The ease with which vaginal cells can be separated from sperm cells makes DNA fingerprinting a powerful technique for investigating rape. In addition, DNA remains stable for years and in blood it can be a reliable long-term indicator of an individual. Bacteria do not affect DNA so that band patterns remain unchanged.

SOME BODY FLUIDS OTHER THAN BLOOD

There are specific and fairly accurate tests available to find out if a particular fluid is saliva, sweat or urine. The difficulty arises with semen and vaginal secretions. The presence of sperm cells, evidence of the male ejaculate, can be detected by microscopic means. But until recently there has been no test for liquid semen that did not include vaginal secretions. Both contain chemicals that appear to a greater or lesser extent in the other. Brentamine tests the high acid phosphatase content of semen to give a colour reaction. However, this enzyme also occurs in vaginal secretions, but to a lesser extent. Within the past few years a protein, designated P 30, has been identified as occurring only in seminal fluid. Now apparently there is a reliable way of finding out if a particular fluid actually contains seminal fluid. Absence of sperm does not, in this age of the 'operation' or the 'snip', indicate absence of seminal fluid.

A problem

Research into P 30, as with research into DNA fingerprinting on sperm etc, requires raw materials. Before any procedure can be accepted as standard forensic practice, intensive research has to be carried out. Who then will volunteer as donors?

> Unlike research into alcohol and its effects, people do not readily come forward to provide 'samples' of one sort or another.

In the end the researchers and their friends, that can be persuaded, have to rely on their own resources to advance the cause of science. The rewards for any such services rendered are never disclosed. Blood that is taken for research must now be free of AIDS and Hepatitis B. One cannot, as in the old days, merely take samples from a host of medical students — who have always been among the best of bleeders.

BLOOD SPOT DISTRIBUTION

Frequently an assault — particularly a savage one — results in considerable spillage of blood. Spots can be distributed liberally around nearby walls and the ceiling. Also a person who is bleeding leaves a trail as he or she attempts to move from the scene. Studying the distribution of blood spots and drops can be helpful in unravelling, or confirming, the sequence of events. This in turn might point to the identity of the assailant. It is a lengthy, painstaking business and requires immense enthusiasm. At the superficial level of a quick survey there is about it a strong hint of Sherlock Holmes. The main requirements are common sense and elementary mathematics.

The width and length of a blood spot reveals the angle at which it struck the surface; the length and direction of the 'tail' indicates velocity and direction respectively. The distance between large spots on the floor (if they can be detected on the carpet) shows the speed of travel, and perhaps height, of an injured person. The number and size of blood spots give some indication of the type of blow inflicted and the weapon used. A fine spray of small spots represents a blow, probably dealt with savage

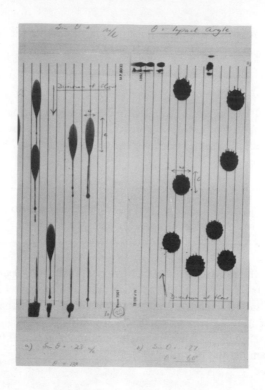

Figure 3.6 *The angle of impact.*
The distribution and shape of blood spots on a wall or ceiling can give clues to the sequence of events during a violent assault. Early forensic scientists asked the question — from the shape and size of the actual spots can the angle of impact be reliably calculated? The answer can only be found by experiment. The photograph shows the results of such an experiment. Blood was dropped from a known height on to cardboard inclined at a known angle. On the left the cardboard was fixed at an angle of 15° to the upright; on the right it was 60°. Calculations based on the dimensions of the spots gave 13° and 60° respectively. So, from measurements on the spots the angle of impact can be reliably calculated.

force, to the head with a blunt instrument. A profusion of blood usually means that the flow ruptures a large blood vessel. Drops propelled at an angle to strike the walls and ceiling suggest the circular motion of a sharp, maybe heavily stained, weapon such as a knife. A few deductions from close observation can help to reconstruct the course of a violent action or actions.

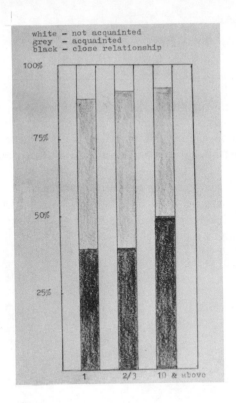

white — not acquainted
grey — acquainted
black — close relationship

Figure 3.7 *Crimes of passion.*
This bar graph summarises a research project carried out to investigate violence against the person. The numbers along the horizontal axis — 1, 2/3, 10, etc. — represent the number of injuries sustained by victims of attack with sharp instruments such as knives.

The left-hand bar indicates that when only one injury was inflicted, the victim was acquainted with his or her attacker in almost 90 per cent of cases studied. Nearly half the attackers were well known to the victims. The other bars show a similar pattern.

In general, it appears that the closer the acquaintance the more the blows/ slashes delivered. This may well be due to panic when blood starts to flow. Many attackers bitterly regret their actions 'in the heat of the moment' and some take their own lives in remorse.

It has been stated by some forensic authorities that "the most savage violence is in the home; the most common weapon is a kitchen knife and the most likely time of the year is January."

Whether the Resource Input to Evidential Value quotient is justified in blood spot distribution remains a matter of debate. This is good forensic jargon that quite simply means:

> Is the value of the results I am likely to get worth the effort I have
> to put in?

This is a problem in all forensic work. There is too much to do and not enough time to do it. A Scene of Crime Officer on the spot can decide what investigations are needed, or indeed are possible. Someone, at some time, has to establish priorities and make the final decision about what actually is done.

Selection of specimens for scientific examination is vital and, in most incidents, can only be done once. An experienced Laboratory Liaison Officer, responsible for examining major crime scenes, commented "if you send garbage in, you can only expect garbage out."

4 The Slog of Particulate Matter, Hair and Fibres

Apart from the body fluids, there are two types of trace evidence exchanged at the scene of a crime:

(a) Biological material that can be hair, natural and man-made fibres, fragments of wood, cigarette ash, pollen, bits of plants and portions of insects. The latter, when found in a drugs haul, might give valuable clues about the country of origin.

(b) Chemical particles that include bits of paint, glass, synthetic rubber, dried ink, dried oil, soil components, drug particles and residues left by explosions and the discharge of firearms.

Particulate matter is made up of tiny particles and these can be either biological or chemical.

The evidence exchanged at most scenes of crime is a mixture of the chemical and biological. The impact of a moving vehicle with a pedestrian usually leaves hair and fibres (also blood) on the automobile and paint, glass and maybe other synthetic materials on the victim.

Searching for, and examining, particulate evidence requires time, patience and care. Success needs a sharp eye and a slice or two of luck. In order to keep the forensic scientist on his or her toes a system of Quality Assurance is operated. Blind, or unknown, items are slipped in among the real ones.

The basic aim of investigating trace evidence is to provide as much information as possible and to link suspect samples with control samples. A suspect sample is one under investigation and about which information is sought. Frequently it is found at the crime scene. A control, against which a suspect is compared, is a sample whose origin and properties are known. Close similarity points to the fact that the suspect and the control came from the same source. The information thus obtained might link a particular person to a particular crime scene. Alternatively, the information might establish that a particular person had nothing to do with the crime scene.

The questions that the scientist investigating particulate trace evidence asks are:

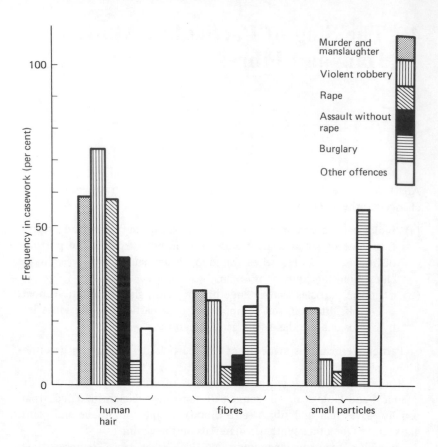

Figure 4.1 *A histograph that shows the relationship between the frequency with which three types of trace evidence occurs in casework, and various criminal offences. Like most statistical displays, the stark facts conceal the 'real stories'.*

A large percentage of trace evidence exchanged during violence against the person is human hair. Most, but not all, can be torn out by the assailant or victim. Hair is easy to grasp for the purpose of forceful manipulation. Other fibres – natural and man-made – are not so readily exchanged during personal violence. This is in spite of the fact that clothing is likely to be wrenched or torn.

Forceful entry into property usually means some distribution of small fragments of glass, paint, wood, etc., more than other trace evidence.

Other offences, the large majority of which are those that breach the Road Traffic Acts, again lead to exchange of small fragments, particularly paint and glass. These are usually found on the victim after impact with a moving vehicle. Significantly, more fibres than hairs are left on the automobile. Clothes are perhaps more exposed than hair and are thus more likely to be torn by hard edges around lights and bumpers.

52

What size is it?
How can one find and then collect it?
How can it be isolated from other traces?
How can it best be inspected and then, if necessary, be analysed?
What relevance has it to the enquiry in progress?

When examining an item for bits and pieces, or particulate matter, a primary consideration for the searching scientist is — What am I actually looking for? To start and continue with the aim of 'merely finding out what is there' would be time consuming and, in the long run, bewildering.

The situation confronting the searcher after particles is similar to that facing the person engaged in pure research. This type of research implies a strong underlying motive of 'Let us see what we can see'. The mind, even a fertile one, can only take this in small doses, simply because there is no overall direction to guide thought or action. Most research, pure or applied, has a definite aim. Certain results are looked for and quite possibly expected. If they do not materialise there is the temptation to fabricate them. A completely open mind is an impossibility and unbridled curiosity leads to madness.

The scientist inspecting a garment for particulate trace evidence needs to have some idea of what to look for. Efforts can then be concentrated in a definite direction. This means that the searcher must have some knowledge of the circumstances from which the suspect items came.

A person who illegally enters private property by forcing a window frame and then smashing a pane of glass is likely to carry away trace evidence of glass, paint and wood. If apprehended soon afterwards some of these fragments might remain about his or her person. These particles would be the main target of an inspection of garments or footwear. If it is known that the intruder trod in some flour then detection of this would be valuable evidence. If this fact is not recorded, the searcher has to resolve the problem — 'This white powder, has it any significance and do I devote time to it?'

At all times after collection, the integrity and continuity of each and every sample and item must be maintained. Integrity means that the specimen arrives at its destination exactly as it was dispatched — no damage has occurred. Continuity means that no contamination occurs during the passage of the sample; care must be taken to ensure that specimens for examination are correctly sealed, labelled and signed for. A forensic scientist would refuse to examine a specimen that he or she thinks has been contaminated or affected in some way. Unless this integrity and continuity are strictly maintained, the evidence obtained is not reliable for presentation in court.

An alert barrister, during his cross-examination, would make 'mince-meat' of both the evidence and the witness who gave it.

Trace evidence and the facts that it reveals, is mostly circumstantial. This means that it is not conclusive and supporting evidence is needed from other sources to eliminate as much doubt as possible.

RECOVERING TRACE EVIDENCE

Before any particulate matter, hairs or fibres can be examined in the laboratory, it/they must be removed and transferred from the crime scene. Often entire garments are transported in sealed containers or bags made of paper or plastic. Removal of trace items in the laboratory can be done by physically picking the items from the background material. Among the methods employed are the use of forceps, brushing into varying sized dishes or on to paper, or the application of suction from a hoover. When suspects or victims undress they normally stand on a clean sheet of paper to collect any debris.

Hairs and fibres can be lifted by the use of adhesive tape. The difficulty with taping is that often vast amounts of background fibres are lifted with the target ones. Also the adhesive itself can interfere with further procedures, such as gas chromatography. Recently a device using the pull of static electricity has been tried for lifting trace evidence. Both the previous disadvantages are remedied but, as is usual with innovations, the lifting efficiency is reduced.

Unlike trace fluids, particulate matter can be manipulated physically before any chemical analysis. The most important instrument for identification and non-destructive examination is the light microscope and its modifications. The humble magnifying glass also has its uses in the preliminaries – as the master sleuth himself realised.

"For a long time Holmes remained there, turning over the leaves and dried sticks, gathering up what seemed to me to be dust into an envelope, and examining with his lens not only the ground, but even the bark of the tree as far as he could reach." A. Conan Doyle

Figure 4.2 *Looking to the future.*
The photograph shows the dust mark lifter being used in research. The aim is to find out if it can separate and lift trace evidence from clothing more efficiently than the present taping method. The principle is to make use of the electrostatic forces of attraction between the traces — slivers of glass, particles of paint, hair, fibres — and an insulator.
On the left is the generator that can impart a charge to the insulator from 100 to 25 000 volts. On the right is a pullover on which glass and a few hairs have been placed. Below this is the earth plate connected to the generator. Spread over the pullover is the insulator, on which rests the probe for imparting the charge. The insulator is coloured black underneath so that lifted particles etc. show up well. A thin metallic conducting layer on the top of the insulator ensures an even spread of the electrostatic charge. A zoom stereo microscope, used for counting the particles and hairs put on and lifted off, is not shown.
This method of trace recovery will only be accepted if statistics indicate its superiority over the present taping method.
As many results as possible have to be obtained from both methods. The mean, or average, percentage recovery of all the traces from several garments must be calculated. These garments have to be those normally worn by criminals — fur coats were not included. These means are then subjected to t-tests to find out if one method is significantly better than the other.

Microscopes are of two kinds — those that use light in the visible range and those that use a stream of electrons. The vast majority of trace particles or fibres can, after screening under the microscope, be passed unchanged for further analysis. Some kind of chromatography, infra red-spectrometry or X-ray diffraction are secondary procedures. Mass spectrometry can also be employed. Stained material, such as sperm cells, are however changed by examination under the microscope and cannot be 'used' further.

RESOLUTION OF THE MICROSCOPE

> The most important aspect of any microscope — electron or light — is its resolution.

This is the ability to distinguish clearly two closely situated spots or points. Short wavelengths give better resolution than the longer wavelengths. Good resolution means that high magnification can be used to advantage.

PHASE CONTRAST

Two modifications make the light microscope even more useful from the forensic point of view. Firstly, phase contrast enables the observer to see clearly a small transparent object with similar refractive properties to that of the background medium. The most common transparent material examined is glass from road accidents and break-ins.

The measure of how a transparent material bends light rays that pass through it, is known as its refractive index, or RI. The glass refracts, or bends, transmitted light waves that are then 'out of step' with those that pass straight through the background medium. These two sets of waves, now with an optical path difference (OPD), are brought to a focus in the eye. The contrast between object and background is then clear. Using this phenomenon, the refractive index of any sliver of glass can be found.

The glass is immersed in oil, which is heated. The refractive index (RI) of the oil falls as the temperature rises. The RI of the glass remains the same. A point is reached when the glass disappears into the oil. This is because, at this point, the RI of the glass and the RI of the oil are identical. Light rays that pass through do not emerge with an optical path difference. When the oil is heated further the glass reappears because there is once again an optical path difference between the emerging rays. The RI of the glass is not the same as that of the oil. The entire procedure can be visualised on a screen and the exact RI of the glass — at the point of its disappearance — can be shown. The variation of the RI of the oil with temperature, accurately known, is incorporated into the monitoring device. One step in the identification of a piece of glass is to find its RI, because each type of glass has its own particular RI.

THE POLARISING MICROSCOPE

The second modification is the use of polarised light, or light whose waves vibrate in one plane or direction only. This enables an observer to detect what happens when such light passes through a hair or fibre.

Often the RI of the fibre in a lengthways direction is different from that in a crossways direction. This is caused by the arrangement of the molecules within the fibre. If polarised light strikes a fibre, particularly at an angle, then two components emerge − a lengthways and a crossways one − whose waves have an optical path difference and are thus 'out of step'. These components are brought to a focus in the eye. The difference between the two refractive indices of a particular fibre is known as its birefringence. A knowledge of birefringence helps to identify a particular fibre.

Birefringence can be calculated from the colour and darkness variation of a fibre if it is rotated when polarised light passes through it.

COMPARISON MICROSCOPY

A further important modification of the ordinary light microscope is the comparison microscope. This is really a joint affair with half the field of view contributed by one microscope and the other half contributed by its twin. Two items − fibres, hairs, bullets, fingerprints − can be compared for matching features (see figures 5.1 and 5.6). One could be the suspect item taken from a scene of crime and the other a control taken from a garment or whatever worn by a person thought to have taken part in the offence. Do they − the suspect and the control − come from the same source? The comparison microscope helps to answer this question.

The colour of suspect and control fibres (or inks) can be compared by an instrument known as a microspectrophotometer. Not surprisingly this is reduced to nanospec! Each fibre is exposed to the colours of the visible spectrum. A 'read out' is obtained of the absorption at each wavelength.

The 'read outs' of the suspect and control fibres can be superimposed and if they fit, they come from the same source. Because of its nature paint reflects rather than absorbs. The 'read out' is a reflectance 'read out'.

The zoom stereo microscope is an excellent tool for examining trace evidence simply because the magnification can be varied gradually. The viewing is done by two eyes instead of one, which gives depth perception. However four hours gazing down this instrument tends to be wearing on the brain cells.

Things are improved by a little of the appropriate refreshment.

THE ELECTRON MICROSCOPE

Compared with the light microscope, the electron microscope is a last resort instrument. Even for simple viewing the object has to be treated in some way and this usually renders it unavailable for further analysis.

An electron microscope can be used in two ways:

(a) the transmission mode (TEM);
(b) the scanning mode (SEM).

In the transmission mode it is used just like a normal light microscope. The resolution given by a stream of electrons is much better than when light is employed. This is because the wavelength of the electron beam is considerably shorter than that of visible light. Fine detail is thus clear even under

Figure 4.3 *Evidence from the infinitesimally small (courtesy of the* ▶ *Metropolitan Police Forensic Laboratory).*
The photograph was taken by an electron microscope and shows a minute globule of metal embedded in a banknote. The note was recovered after a safe had been opened with oxy-acetylene flame equipment. The metal was identified, and a link with the safe established, using a microprobe attached to the microscope. This probe picks up X-rays that are emitted from elements when they are scanned with a high-energy electron beam. Each element emits its own characteristic X-rays. Down to 10^{-14} g of a metal in a 1 µm region can be detected and identified in this way.
The graph, or read-out, is a typical X-ray emission spectrum of gun shot residues. Identifying the elements can give a good idea of the type of ammunition used. Along the horizontal, or x, axis is X-ray energy, which is equivalent to the wavelength emitted. The y, or vertical, axis represents abundance based on X-ray counts. The peaks, large or small, for any element always occur in the same place, or wavelength. The positions of antimony, lead and barium are shown.

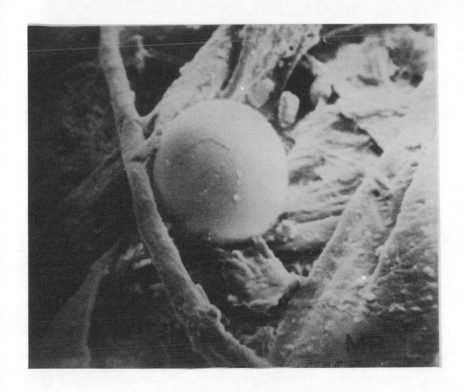

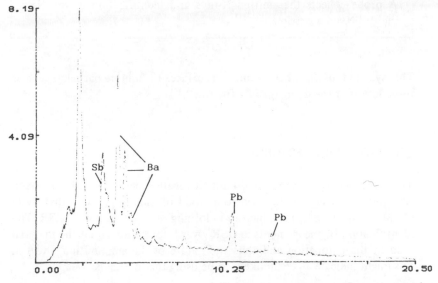

the high magnifications (half a million or more) of the electron microscope. In fact, maybe surprisingly, little use is made of the electron microscope in its transmission mode in the forensic laboratory.

> Its value lies in the scanning mode.

If the surface of a specimen being examined is coated with a very thin layer of metal, such as gold, this surface becomes conducting. The topography, or 'humps and bumps' of the surface, can then be studied. This is done by focusing the electron beam over each portion of surface in a regular, predetermined manner.

When electrons strike a particular element on the surface of a specimen, or item, one result is an emission of X-rays. Another is the release of back scatter electrons. Each element that is hit by the electrons has its own particular X-ray emission pattern. A record of this emission pattern, or emission spectrum, reveals the identity of the element present on the surface under inspection. Coating with gold, to study topography, would prevent this. Surfaces can be scanned with the beam of electrons (hence the scanning mode) for X-rays and back scatter electrons.

> A probe collects the emitted X-rays and identification of the elements becomes possible.

This system is useful when examining surfaces for minute particles, such as those left after the discharge of a firearm.

GUNSHOT RESIDUES (GSR)

The working parts of a firearm do not fit together perfectly and the person who pulls the trigger is exposed to a cloud of minute particles that fly in all directions. Hands, face, hair and clothing are spattered with GSR. The identification of the elements in GSR gives information about the material used in the detonation and thus the nature of the ammunition. In turn, this might indicate a person likely to be using that particular weapon.

60

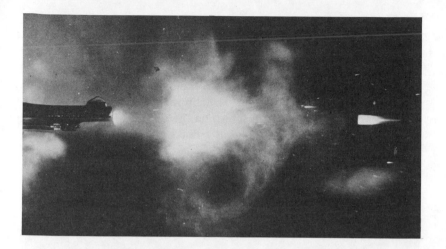

Figure 4.4 *The origin of Gun Shot Residues (GSR) (courtesy of the Metropolitan Police Forensic Laboratory).*
This trick of high-speed photography clearly shows the cloud of minute particles that accompanies a detonation in the breech of a revolver. These particles lodge in the clothing and on the skin of the person who pulls the trigger. Some particles even enter the nose and can be recovered from the nasal passages.
The emerging bullet is on the right of the photograph.

> The modern criminal, alive to the dangers of detection resulting from detonation residues, often wears a complete protective suit for activities such as safe blowing. At the end of the 'job' the entire outfit, with its tall tale residues, is left behind.

Explosion or gunshot residues can be removed from clothing or skin by swabbing with a suitable solvent. A small portion of the swabbings is then subjected to analysis by thin layer, or gas, chromatography. This second method of analysis or examination is essential to all forensic work. In this instance of GSR the information gathered from the scanning electron microscope and probe is then corroborated — or not as the case may be.

> Whenever possible the forensic scientist has to confirm one test with another, preferably of a different kind.

INFRA-RED SPECTROMETRY

The detection of chemical compounds in dyes, drugs, etc. can be effected by the use of infra-red spectrometry. Pigment extracted from a small portion of suspect fibre, for example, is exposed to the sequence of wavelengths in the infra-red spectrum. The absorbance of these various wavelengths by the extracted dye is shown on the output of modern chemical machinery — the graphical 'read out'. Peaks indicate high absorbance, troughs show low absorbance. Every chemical has its own characteristic infra-red 'read out' which is the result of infra-red waves interacting with the chemical groups within each molecule. Comparison with a library of known 'read outs' can identify an unknown substance. As would be expected, experienced operators can confidently interpret the complex wave patterns at a glance.

MASS SPECTROMETRY

One of the most expensive, and thus one of the most highly regarded, methods of detecting and identifying compounds is the mass spectrometer

Figure 4.5 *The mass spectrometer — a means of identification.* ➤
Often the mass spectrometer is used to identify components of a mixture that have previously been separated. The separating system can be GC or HPLC.
In the diagram, the 'treatment' chamber is where the molecules of the eluent, or compound emerging from the separating column, are made into charged particles, or fragments. The method most commonly used is bombardment with electrons, or electron impact (EI). The electrostatic analyser is a filter device. An electrostatic field only allows the passage of particles that exceed a certain energy level; the rest fall by the wayside. The magnetic analyser sorts out the charged particles, or fragments, according to their mass and charge. The lighter particles are deflected more than the heavier ones.
The graph shows the end result (the 'print out') of passing cocaine molecules through the mass spectrometer. Such a 'print out' could be used as a control when investigating unknown substances for cocaine.
Along the horizontal, or x, axis is the mass-to-charge ratio of the fragments striking the receptors. This ratio is expressed as m/z or m/e. The y, or vertical, axis represents relative intensity or abundance — in effect, how much there is of that particular fragment.
According to the method of bombardment, or 'treatment', a characteristic pattern of vertical lines is printed out. It is this pattern that is important in identifying a particular compound. The line at m/z 182 is the molecular ion of cocaine.

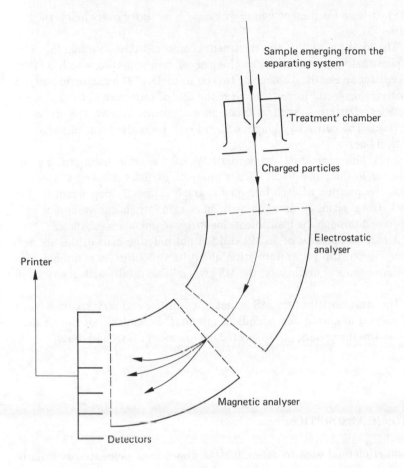

Sample emerging from the separating system

'Treatment' chamber

Charged particles

Printer

Electrostatic analyser

Magnetic analyser

Detectors

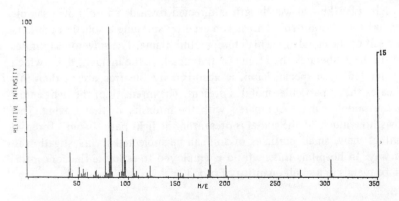

(MS). It is an instrument whose awesome complexity overwhelms the layman.

The ideal product of the treatment chamber is the molecular ion. This implies that very little has been chipped off each molecule, which is intact except for an electrical charge or two on its surface. The magnetic analyser generates magnetic forces that alter the line of movement of the charged particles. Detectors, such as electron multipliers, receive the deflected particles. The customary graphical 'read out' takes the form of a series of vertical lines.

Each line represents many particles of the same mass striking the detector in the same place. Such a group of particles is called a 'species'. Thus the position of each line on the graph is directly dependent on the mass. Once again, comparison with lines made when known compounds are passed through the instrument, identifies an unknown substance.

A shrewd operator of an MS can tell not only the mass of the 'species' emerging but can gain information about its structure. As is normal with modern chemical machinery, the MS gives reliable results with a very small input.

The great benefit of the MS is that it is sensitive and very accurate when identifying unknown compounds in mixtures. Forensically it can be used to confirm the presence of suspected compounds in GSR and drugs.

ATOMIC ABSORPTION

Another method used to determine the presence of elements, particularly metals, is atomic absorption. This is based on the fact that free atoms of metals absorb certain wavelengths of visible light.

Light of a known wavelength is directed towards an unknown sample that has been 'atomised'. This is achieved by spraying a solution containing a salt of the metal into a high temperature flame. The solvent evaporates and the heat liberates the atoms of the metal. If the incident light, which is generated by a special lamp, is absorbed by the free atoms then this indicates that a particular metal is present. The intensity of the light entering the sample can be compared with the intensity of that leaving. This shows how much of the metal is present in the light path. From a forensic point of view, small particles of soil can be subjected to investigation in this way. In hospitals this method is employed to estimate the concentration of metals in a small quantity of blood.

X-RAY DIFFRACTION

Rays of any kind – light, X-rays, beams of electrons – are changed when they strike elements or compounds that are 'in their way'. When X-rays are trained into a crystal, the X-rays are diffracted. They emerge from the crystal at an angle to the line or plane of entry. The direction of the diffraction is characteristic of the arrangement of the atoms within the crystal.

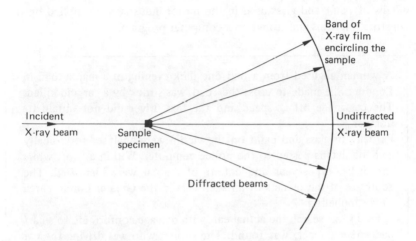

A developed X-ray plate showing the two apertures for X-rays to enter and leave and the diffraction pattern of the specimen:

Figure 4.6 *X-ray diffraction.*

Basically the diffraction, or deflection, is because the atoms within the crystal are arranged in a definite, regular three-dimensional manner (an example of the orderliness of Nature). There is no change of wavelength when the X-rays are diffracted by the crystal. The energy of the incident beam is the same as that of the diffracted beams.

Diffraction patterns that result from a particular crystal are 'finger-prints' of that crystalline structure. When compared with known diffraction 'fingerprints', a small fragment of a crystalline substance can be identified chemically.

X-ray diffraction is useful forensically because it is a process that does not destroy the target specimen. Also it needs minute quantities with no preliminary treatment. Provided they are of a crystalline nature, compounds can be identified as well as elements, for example, slivers of metal. X-ray diffraction can be used to identify the salt derivatives of drugs and the various additives such as sugar. It can also be employed to analyse and compare paint samples from break-ins and from road accidents. All the details of paint and glass used in the motor industry are supplied by the construction firms and stored on a computer program.

A woman alighted from a taxi one dark evening in a major road in London. She made to cross the road, was struck by a car and killed. The car made off at speed and the taxi driver did not obtain its number.

Particles of glass and paint on the victim were analysed forensically and the details passed to the police computer. Within a short while the make, type, year and colour of the car were identified. The addresses of the owners of all such cars in the Greater London area were supplied.

After a short search the actual car, with damage conforming to a car/ pedestrian impact, was found. The owner, who was driving the car on the evening of the accident, was apprehended.

In most circumstances, trace evidence is lost quickly obeying the principle 'easy come, easy go'. After an exchange, a large percentage can be lost during the first hour or so of wear — if the evidence is on a garment. After a day little is left, although a few particles may stay for days, maybe weeks. These however, could be difficult to retrieve as they would be lodged in seams or joins. The longer after the exchange an item or specimen is inspected, the greater the input of time and effort to obtain useful information. There comes a point when this input is just not worthwhile.

5   Marks

There are words in the English language that are best left to speak for themselves. Their shortness and simplicity defy precise definition. 'Mark' is such a word. Everyone really knows what a mark is and one reputable dictionary states 'Mark — making a mark. . ." etc. So a mark is a mark.

Marks are made when surfaces interact. Both surfaces are affected in some way but usually the mark on one is more obvious than the mark on the other. Most marks are irreversible in that, once made, the surface cannot be restored to its exact former state. An impression, on the other hand, implies that the surface can return to its former state — or almost.

Not only is it forensic scientists who examine items for marks and trace evidence. Others also have alert eyes and logical minds.

A farmer, known to the author, developed a lucrative business of considerable benefit to himself but to the detriment of the Inland Revenue. He found that wealth and power can be an effective aphrodisiac. One evening, in the heat of the moment, he forgot to remove his shirt. He also ignored the fact that cosmetics make a clear mark on clean white fabric.

The lady of his house prided herself on her ability to 'hold her man'. When organising the laundry the mark came to her notice. A comparison of the suspect mark with the controls of her selection did not reveal an exact match. Another source was involved. Further scrutiny led to the detection of trace evidence on other garments.

The authorities received an anonymous 'tip off' and the farmer's fortunes declined abruptly.

The type and extent of a particular mark is determined by:

(a) the nature of the surface on which the mark is made;
(b) the nature of the surface that makes the mark;

(c) the energy of interaction, which includes the pressure applied and the time of its application.

The violent manipulation of an iron bar against a door post makes a mark vastly different from the impression of a finger on a silk handkerchief. The most obvious marks are those made with metal tools or accessories, particularly those that leave a characteristic pattern such as screws or drills.

One forensic value of a mark is the possibility of obtaining a 'physical fit' — see figure 1.4.

If pieces of wood are wrenched out of a door post or window frame in the course of a break-in, then one, or several, of the fragments will fit back perfectly into the damaged area. Similarly a piece of glass can fit a broken pane, or a flake of paint fit neatly into an area from which paint has been chipped away. A person found with a splinter of wood, or piece of glass, that 'physically fits' a mark at a scene of crime needs a very convincing story to explain away such a coincidence.

MARKS AND FIREARMS

Microscopically the matching of two items for a 'physical fit', or identical marking, is done by the comparison microscope — already mentioned in chapter 4. Marks on bullets and cartridges are good examples.

When a gun is fired, marks are made on the bullet as it travels along the barrel. There are ridges lining the gun barrel and the spiral nature of these imparts a spin to the bullet. This rifling, as it is called, makes horizontal scratches on the bullet. The rifling of each gun barrel is unique to that gun. A comparison of two bullets — suspect and control — fired from the same gun reveals identical rifling marks. These can be matched by placing the two bullets under a comparison microscope. A control bullet is obtained by firing the gun into water. In this way the marks on the bullet are left intact. The suspect bullet is taken from a victim or at the scene of a crime.

Marks, also unique to a particular gun, are made on the cartridge cases. The reaction to the release of the bullet causes the cartridge to press hard against the breech. Marks of compression result. The firing pin strikes the

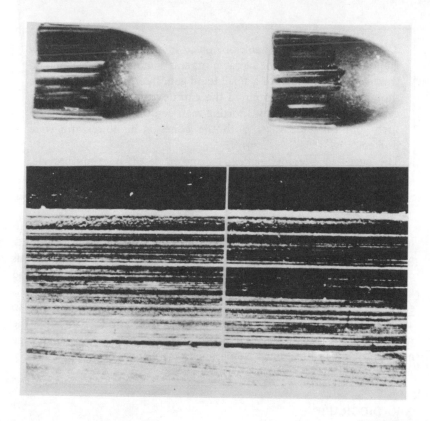

Figure 5.1 *The signature on the bullet (courtesy of the Metropolitan Police Forensic Laboratory).*
The upper part of this photograph shows two bullets, the suspect on the left and the control on the right. Both have obvious rifling marks along them.
The lower part is the result of placing both bullets under the comparison microscope. The match of the marks, which can never be absolutely perfect, is sufficiently close to indicate that both bullets were fired by the same gun.

detonating cap in a certain spot — frequently not dead centre. In an automatic or magazine type weapon the cartridge is extracted from the breech and an extractor mark results. Similarly the ejection of the cartridge from the breech causes an ejector mark. Microscopic examination of an available suspect cartridge with a control can reveal that both were fired from the same weapon.

Certain elementary facts cannot be ignored when using a firearm.

Two men rushed into a bank obviously intent on 'picking up a few grand' quickly. One carried a sawn off shot gun in his right hand and waved it in the manner of a small hand gun. In order to reinforce the shouted commands, he pointed the gun upwards and fired into the ceiling. The recoil, as any sporting man could have told him, from such guns can be savage. Both the bones in his lower arm were broken.

The men fled — empty handed — and made off on a motorcycle. Within a few hours they were in police custody.

Many marks are not evident to the naked eye in reflected or in transmitted light. Either the mark is too faint or the contrast with the background, particularly a dark one, is not sufficiently pronounced. Rising to this challenge to reveal the 'invisible', the scientists have devised ways and means of showing up these marks. Most methods require that the surface is exposed to some form of strong radiation. The simplest method is to arrange for a beam of bright light — from a strong torch — to strike the surface at an angle. Under these conditions, shadows show up that were not formed under direct light. Sometimes a mark appears.

X-RADIOGRAPHY

X-rays can be used to show up otherwise 'invisible' marks. The principle is that different materials, or different thicknesses of the same material, absorb X-rays by different amounts. The contrast obtained by this differential absorbance, and thus reflection, can be recorded on film. Two types of X-ray are employed:

(a) 'Hard' X-rays of short wavelength can penetrate plate steel an inch thick. These X-rays can be used to examine damaged vehicle tyres for marks that might give clues to the true events of a road accident. A firearm can be exposed to 'hard' X-rays to reveal external marks that could establish its whereabouts at the time it was discharged. Diamond substitutes absorb more of these X-rays than do genuine 'stones' (being made of carbon), and scanning with hard X-rays is a useful technique for examining rapidly large quantities of suspect diamonds.

(b) 'Soft' X-rays have a longer wavelength than 'hard' X-rays. They are less penetrating and are used on less robust targets. Bank notes, stamps and documents of various natures are subjected to soft X-rays. Com-

70

parison of a suspect document with an original, or genuine, document can, under 'soft' X-rays reveal a forgery.

Some £5 notes were detected as forgeries because the radiographs resulting from 'soft' X-ray exposure showed a difference in the composition of the ink. The design, water marks and metal strip were all exactly as they should be. By eye it was not possible to detect any irregularity. But the ink used in genuine bank notes has a metal base whereas that used in the forgeries had a carbon base. The radiographs of a suspect and a genuine note showed different design patterns because the inks absorbed 'soft' X-rays differently.

THE LASER

A recent development in the detection of 'invisible' marks and impressions is the laser.

A laser, acronym for Light Amplification by Stimulated Emission of Radiation, produces a beam of radiation that is monochromatic, coherent, collimated and maybe polarised into the bargain.

Put more simply, monochromatic means that the emerging radiation is of one wavelength only. There are few, if any, other wavelengths present. Most other systems that generate radiation produce a principal wavelength with varying amounts of others that tend to contaminate the main component.

Laser radiation is usually light from within the visible spectrum (red to blue) but there are lasers that produce infra-red and ultra-violet beams.

Coherence describes the situation when all the waves are 'in step'. They all vibrate in harmony rather than the peaks of some waves overlapping the troughs of others.

Collimated refers to the fact that all the 'in step' waves are travelling in precisely the same direction. There are no waves going at an angle to the direction of flow. The implication of this is that a lot of energy can be concentrated in a narrow beam — a fact that is used in medicine. The polarisation, as with the polarisation in a microscope, means that all the waves, with their troughs and peaks coinciding, are vibrating in the same plane.

71

The long words describing the laser are not too difficult to understand. One application of lasers in forensic work is based on the phenomenon of fluorescence. If a beam of coloured light — blue for instance — hits a surface, quite often substances in that surface will fluoresce.

> The impact of a certain colour light causes radiation of a longer wavelength to be given off.

Thus a ray of blue light striking a fluorescent substance might cause the emission of green, or even red, light in response. Some substances do not fluoresce in blue light but do so in red. In this case the emitted radiation is of the shorter infra-red wavelengths. The shift in wavelength between the incident and emitted light is called the Stokes shift. Many substances do not fluoresce at all.

Ageing may cause a substance to change its fluorescence response. A surface may thus contain several substances that can be distinguished by fluorescence; one may fluoresce in the blue, another in the red and a third in the ultra-violet. Fluorescence can be used to discriminate between substances in a surface without in any way affecting the surface.

When a laser is turned off the fluorescence gradually goes, or decays. Laser illumination given in pulses, or short bursts, can differentiate between two substances, both of which might fluoresce in the blue but show different decay times.

Because a laser beam is monochromatic and coherent, fluorescence from a surface is clear and sharp. Fluorescence in laser systems is much clearer than in others. Scanning a surface with different colour laser beams can reveal marks. A name or a number on a travelling bag, completely invisible to the naked eye or any other illuminating device, can show up under laser scanning. One laser expert stated that he much prefers murders to be committed, and reported, in the evening. He then has the opportunity to scan the entire premises with his laser 'gear' during the night, free from outside interference. By morning he will have a record of tell tale marks on walls, floors, etc. that could be of forensic importance.

> This is the investigative area of forensic science that is the more interesting. Corroborative work has maybe not the same excitement.

A laser beam can be used in the process of holography for showing marks. A single original beam is split into two components. One of these is diverted on to the surface under examination while the other proceeds straight on. After bouncing off the target surface, the beams are brought to a focus on a screen.

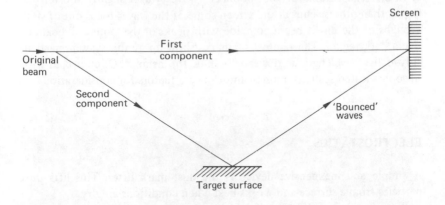

Figure 5.2 *The holograph.*

Figure 5.3 *The footprint on the carpet (courtesy of the Metropolitan Police Forensic Laboratory).*
A holograph of a footprint. It is probable that this mark is so faint that only laser interference using the holograph technique will show it up.

Distances are arranged so that there will be no interference, and no dark and light patterns, on the screen if the second component strikes a completely smooth surface. At the screen the two beams are in phase as each wave peak coincides with other wave peaks. If, however, there are irregularities, or marks, on the surface then these show up on the screen because of interference. Some of the 'bounced' waves travel slightly shorter distances than others. Thus at the screen some of the waves focus out of step. Troughs of the direct beam coincide with peaks of the 'bounced' beam to give a dark region. The faintest of marks show up by this system, particularly if the wavelength used is short — blue for instance. Of course, as with all sophisticated systems, money and time are factors for consideration.

ELECTROSTATICS

A simple and inexpensive device is the dust mark lifter. This lifts dust particles from a surface and works best when conditions are dry.

The particles are lifted uniformly in the pattern in which they settled after a disturbance — by a car tyre or someone's boot. The operating principle is that an electrical insulator, coloured black, is gently placed over the area under scrutiny. A large voltage, up to 15000 volts (15 kV), is applied to this insulator. Against this black background the dust pattern shows up clearly when the voltage is switched off and the insulator removed for inspection.

Any marks, such as tyre marks, handprints, footprints, etc. show up well even if the total lift of dust particles does not exceed 25 per cent.

The essence of the dust mark lifter is the even nature of the lift over the surface of the insulator. This device has been modified, although operating on the same principle, to show indentations on paper.

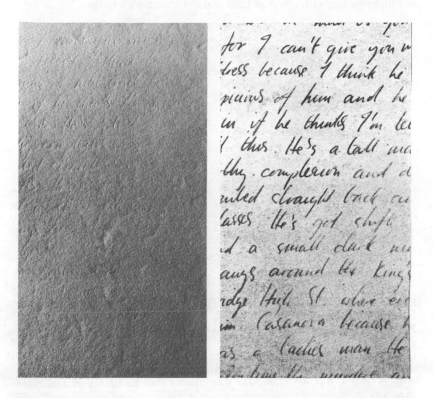

Figure 5.4 *Revelations of static electricity (courtesy of Foster and Freeman).*

On the left is a piece of paper, or document, that has been photographed under light trained obliquely across its surface. It is the lower sheet of two, and indentations are vaguely visible. These marks were made by someone writing on the upper sheet.

On the right is a photograph of the same indentations, taken after electrostatic treatment, using an ESDA (electrostatic detection apparatus) device. A polymer film is placed over the target document and pulled down tightly on to it by suction. The two surfaces in close contact are then charged up. The polymer film is 'developed' by pouring Xerox toner over it. This toner is secured on to the film by adhesive plastic. The polymer/toner/plastic sandwich is peeled off and the indented writing is clearly revealed on the underside. The document is left completely unharmed. Exactly how this works is not known.

The interpretation of marks on flesh have to be treated with caution. Flesh, being a soft tissue, changes with time. Despite this, laser scanning and illumination with infra-red light can detect marks on skin.

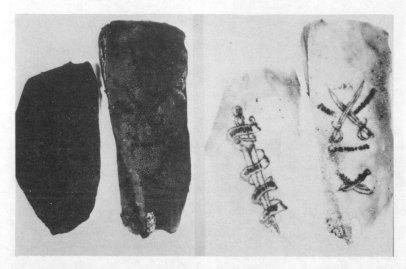

Figure 5.5 *Identification by tattoo (courtesy of the Metropolitan Police Forensic Laboratory).*
The left side of the picture shows two portions of skin of a decomposing body. Marks are visible but not clear.
On the right are the same portions of skin photographed when illuminated with infra-red light. Tattoos show up clearly. This is because the skin reflects this wavelength of light and the chemicals of the tattoo mark absorb it.
By revealing these marks the identity of the dead person was eventually established.

WOUNDS

Perhaps the most identifiable marks made on flesh are those made by teeth (human and animal) and by a weapon that imparts a particular pattern of marks. Attack with a branding iron might leave a characteristic mark — as do love bites. A bite mark, if fresh, can be checked against dentures and dental patterns. In order to check a fairly fresh bite mark against a suspect's teeth, an impression can be made for comparison using the normal dental material. Soil is also a soft material and plaster casts can be made of suspect tyres or footprints. These can be compared with the original, if it is available.

> It is the pattern of a mark on the body that is important.

Knife and bullet wounds tend to have their own characteristics. Often, however, little else can be deduced except 'impact by a sharp or blunt instrument', although bruises can show detail particularly at the edges.

The effects on the human body of a bullet fired from a gun are different from those inflicted by the impact of shot from a shot gun. The presence of gunshot residues and the general appearance of a wound might give an indication of the distance between the muzzle of the gun and the victim. Examining wounds is the task of the pathologist, although the forensic scientist can gain experience in the course of his or her work.

MANUFACTURER'S MARKS

There are marks of forensic value that do not appear as a result of criminal intent. They constitute a kind of preventative means of countering crime. All glass in modern vehicles, particularly the glass of headlamps, is marked by the manufacturer. After an accident, a mark on a fragment of glass retrieved from the scene or found on a victim helps to identify the vehicle. In turn this could lead to the driver, who is usually the owner. It is now common practice to have the car registration number engraved on the glass of each window. This can help with tracing a stolen vehicle, or one that has been altered in some way before it is sold.

Marks can be placed on jewellery to aid identification. With modern methods of electronic storage and recall of information, these deliberately placed manufacturer's marks can be valuable when gaining information about a criminal or traffic offence. Some marks are placed on items merely as a result of the manufacturing process. The tools that make them leave their impression. Screws, nails and wire are marked with characteristic grooves and scratches as they are produced. A box of screws will have closely similar manufacturing marks if they were made consecutively on the same machine. In time these marks change as the machine tools wear.

A person who has used a number of screws to make a false compartment to a case might absently put the remainder of the packet into his pocket. The two sets would be marked almost identically. If this person is now caught and searched, the screws in his pocket would be compared with those in the case. His protestations that the two sets were in no way connected would not sound convincing.

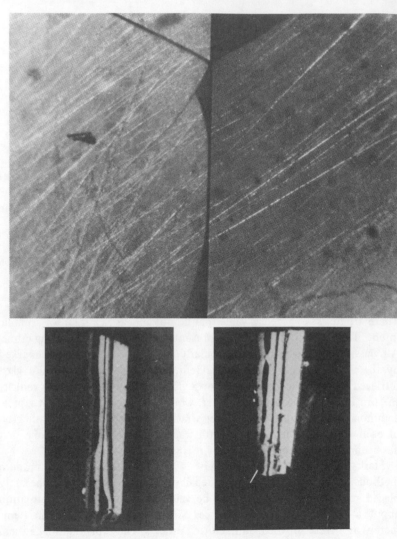

Figure 5.6 *Matching patterns.*

Upper photograph (copyright American Society for Testing and Materials — reproduced with permission): two paint chips, side by side, under the comparison microscope. The one on the left (with the jagged edge) was taken from a suspect; the one on the right was taken from the scene of a break-in.

The scratch patterns match almost exactly. It is highly likely — almost certain — that the two pieces came from the same source.

Lower photograph: a cross-sectional comparison of two flakes of paint. The longer piece was taken from a suspect vehicle and the shorter piece was taken from the victim of an accident. The match is close with respect to the number and width of the layers.

FINGERPRINTS

Probably the most well known mark associated with the criminal scene is a fingerprint. Each individual has a particular pattern of finger and thumb prints, special to himself or herself. These prints are, in effect, the impressions of ridges and furrows formed on the outer skin. All tissue growth and repair is under genetic control, and the fact that each person has a unique fingerprint testifies to the immense variation in the human genetic make up.

Fingerprints, or 'dabs', are left as marks because of the nature of the skin surface. Oils and debris are always on the ridge tops and furrow sides. The merest touch on a window pane, table, garment or whatever means that the ridges make contact. Debris, oil and dead outer cells are left behind. If fine dust is sprinkled on to these remnants, it sticks. The print clearly stands out if the excess dust is blown away. Comparison with known prints can identify an individual and the comparison microscope is used for this purpose. Control prints can be obtained by rolling the end of the finger or thumb in moist black ink. The finger is then pressed on to white paper and the ink from the ridges dries to form the actual print. A genuine match is declared only if there are sixteen identical characteristics shared by suspect and control. The significant points of comparison are the sites of the ridge ends. A genuine match means that both prints — suspect and control — come from the same source, that is, the suspect individual.

Because the debris on the ridges contains proteins and amino acids, a fingerprint on soft material such as paper can be revealed by the application of a protein stain, ninhydrin. The dye is sprayed on to the paper.

Various dyes, notably rhodamine, are taken up by print debris and the dye can be detected and visualised by fluorescence. The dye fluoresces and the background does not. On harder surfaces, laser fluorescence can be used.

Recently a move has been made to computerise the storage, recall and comparison of fingerprints. This would speed up the process considerably.

Since modern examination and survey techniques reveal so much that would otherwise remain 'invisible', it is likely that the famous "every contact leaves a trace" might have to be modified to

> "Every contact leaves a trace and a mark."

Figure 5.7 *The print on the bag — detection (courtesy of the Metropolitan Police Forensic Laboratory).*
The upper part of the photograph shows a plastic bag (containing, among other things, mushrooms) recovered from the scene of a criminal incident. Under normal light nothing incriminating is evident.
The lower part of the photograph shows the same area of the bag subjected to light from a green laser (514.5 nm).
A fingerprint now stands out clearly and the printing on the bag disappears. The white background of the bag has gone black because the material absorbs this wavelength. The mushrooms merely change colour.

Certain evidence, relating to traces and marks, is more convincing, and thus carries more weight, than other evidence. A physical or mechanical fit is particularly significant. An intruder who breaks into private property might take away fragments of paint on his clothing. These fragments will obviously match other bits, taken from the point of entry, with respect to colour and layering. But the chance of such a match occurring at random

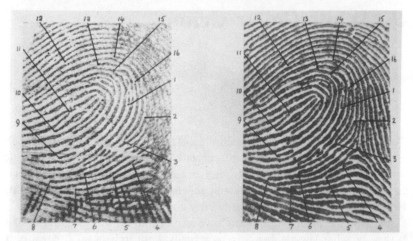

Figure 5.8 *Comparison: matching the fingerprints (courtesy of the Metropolitan Police Forensic Laboratory).*
On the left is the suspect 'print' found at the scene or on a weapon; on the right is the control 'print' from a known individual. The definite match of sixteen distinct points of detail show that almost certainly both prints were made by the same person.

is by no means negligible, simply because anybody can have paint fragments about them. Everyone comes into contact with paint.

In figure 5.6 the true physical fit is achieved by the scratch marks, that are unique to the area of paint from which the two fragments came. In effect, only one tool (handled by one person) could have made marks that fit so well.

Modern scientific instruments are capable of detecting and identifying such minute amounts of target substances that the question must arise – Is a very tiny quantity of any real significance? There can be no doubt about a person being 'in possession of an illegal drug' if he or she is found with 100 g of heroin in an inside pocket. But what if just a few microscopic grains are found? These could have originated from a contaminated paper bag idly picked up, absently stuffed into a pocket and later discarded. Equally these grains could have come from another 100 g 'lot'.

A chance event can invalidate evidence that otherwise would contribute to a convincing case. A well-intentioned police officer may, at one moment, be comforting a rape victim and shortly after may be helping to detain the suspect rapist. A defence counsel would no doubt point out that any fibres and hairs found on the suspect, and shown by scientific tests to match those of the victim, could have been transferred by the officer in the legitimate pursuit of his duty. If possible, precautions have to be taken to avoid such eventualities.

6   White Collar Crime

To the vast majority of people a criminal is, in all probability, a 'thick ape'. He, or very rarely she, breaks into private dwellings, enters banks waving sawn off shot guns, beats up old ladies and anyone else unfortunate enough to be in the way, spits frequently and generally leaves a trail of destruction. He is usually between the ages of twenty and thirty five.

Perhaps the media are in some way responsible for this image, although it may be what law-abiding citizens actually want to believe. The reality is different as affluence increases and technology expands.

THE WHITE COLLAR 'CRIMINAL'

The sums of money handled by ordinary criminals — those that conform to the type — are negligible compared with the vast fortunes amassed by those who embezzle, engage in fraud, take advantage of inside knowledge and manipulate modern electronic devices.

> Back in 1975 a computer fraud involving a million dollars was considered "only a modest haul." What is 'a rake off' now?

Such activities tend not to be regarded as strictly criminal. Rather they fall into the category of ungentlemanly conduct — or at very worst of corruption. The air of respectability that surrounds such proceedings gives rise to the White Collar label.

Those involved often reside in large suburban villas with immaculate lawns and rose gardens; they wear suits with the Savile Row tag; they travel first class and, in some instances, are pillars of the local church. Many possess a University degree. Exposure of a racket sometimes takes the public by surprise as famous names are paraded in the press.

During the investigation of large-scale fraud or insider dealing, only selected items are taken to the forensic laboratory. To inspect the complete financial records of an entire firm, or the computations of an international company, usually needs specialists on the spot. Money that has been 'laundered' or 'salted away' can be difficult to find. The accountants and the systems analysts have to be called in. The hunter and the hunted are equals in expertise and, in the ensuing struggle (or is it a game?), there must be elation at success on either side. As usual, this success is likely to be the result of a few strokes of good fortune.

EXPOSING FORGERIES

Apart from the need to manipulate numbers and computer systems, the scientific investigation of forgery and fraud tends to be directed at three main areas. These have to be carried out in the forensic laboratory:

(a) the analysis and inspection of the background material, which is usually paper;
(b) the comparison of designs made on this background material;
(c) the analysis of chemicals, mostly inks, that make up the patterns or designs.

Paper or cardboard can be smashed up in a blender or mixer and then inspected microscopically. The nature of the fibres that make up the paper can reveal the country of origin. Staining emphasises the contrast between fibres and non-fibres. The fillers that make the gloss of the writing surface can be identified by X-ray diffraction as outlined in chapter 4. The use of X-rays in simple radiography (similar to the X-rays taken in hospital) detect watermarks that are put into paper for security reasons. Bank notes are printed on special paper that, for obvious reasons, is very difficult to obtain.

One of the best 'forgeries' of all time was the Piltdown Man — some fossil remains of an ape/man that seemed to support the idea of descent from a common ancestor. The solid background in this case was bone. Eventually chemical analysis of the individual bones showed that they did not match and could not have come from the same source. Also the analysis did not correspond with that of other bones found in the same rock mineral layer.

When comparing the pattern or design made on the background material, using a full field projector can be better than a comparison microscope. This enables the operator to compare, on a large screen, the suspect and

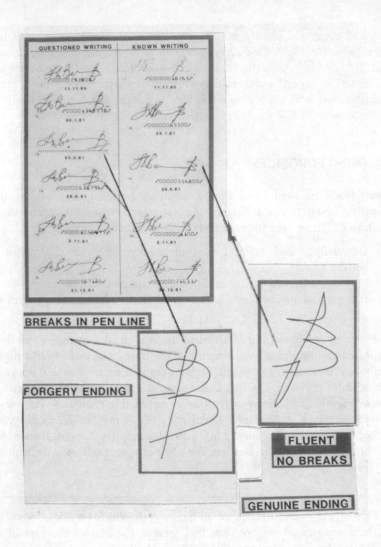

Figure 6.1 *Detecting forgeries. (courtesy of the Metropolitan Police Forensic Laboratory).*

The photograph shows two sequences of a signature placed side by side. On the left are six suspected forgeries; on the right, five known genuine signatures. The lack of fluency shown in the magnified endings indicated that the suspects were indeed forgeries.

In fact this forger successfully 'fiddled' well over a £¼ million before being detected.

Apparently genuine signatures have more variation in form than forced ones. The forger, in an attempt to appear correct, tends to write uniform signatures.

84

control items side by side, or even superimposed. Also the images can be switched from suspect to control at a given speed so that the brain of the observer records a continuous image. Any differences make a direct impression.

Often the detection of forgery means the meticulous comparison of handwriting. Training for this work is arduous, with attention focused on barely perceptible detail. Similarly the matching of a piece of print to a particular typewriter needs a trained eye, although each individual type-writer has its own peculiarities.

Modern word processors that print by the daisy wheel system can probably be identified by the rigorous comparison process. However, the dot matrix 'print outs' may pose difficulties. Informed authorities have stated that the spacing of the dots, and the depth of the impression on the paper, must be characteristic of each individual machine. Modern laser printers are likely to be even more difficult to characterise on an individual basis. Research into this aspect of detecting fraud might prove worthwhile, if distinctly tedious.

The most common chemical used on the background material to make a pattern is an ink of some nature. Detection of a certain type, or even age, of ink can be carried out by processes mentioned in previous chapters, such as colour absorbance by nanospec, fluorescence, analysis using thin layer chromatography or high pressure liquid chromatography, infra-red spectrometry or X-radiography. Perhaps the most vulnerable aspect of the forger's art is the ink, which can be subjected to an extensive battery of chemical tests.

Recently the microtechnologists have developed an automated system for detecting forged signatures – a lucrative area of crime.

Sample signatures (usually six) from an individual are 'read' by a pattern recognition process. The result is a 10-digit number specific to the parent signature. This number can then be printed on a cheque or incorporated into the magnetic strip of a credit card. It can also be stored in a database. A cheque presented at a bank, or a credit card at a shop, is passed through a compact scanning device. A microcomputer compares the number with the accompanying signature. Acceptance or the inability to confirm a correlation is registered within 3 seconds.

This neat system can, it is claimed, detect all 'unseen' forgeries. These make up 95 per cent of total forgeries and occur when a person wipes the signature from a stolen credit card and substitutes his or her own. The original number must be available for comparison. The substitution can be in reverse – a person wipes off his or her own signature and substitutes someone else's.

'Seen' forgeries, where a person copies a signature from a cheque on to another cheque or card, can also be detected. Once again, comparison is impossible without the original number.

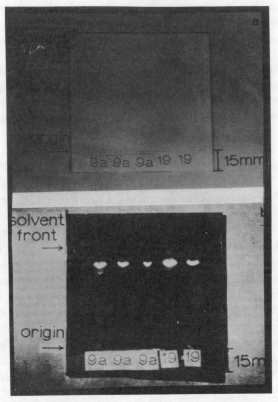

Figure 6.2 *Fluorescence in blue.*
A comparison of two inks – designated respectively 9a and 19 – by thin layer chromatography (TLC). Both specimens of ink have been diluted. The left-hand sample of 9a has been diluted 1 part ink to 100 parts solvent; the centre sample 1 in 500 and the right-hand sample 1 in 1000. The left-hand sample of 19 has been diluted 1 in 100 and the right-hand sample 1 in 500. Small portions, no more than 10 microlitres of each sample, were applied to the line of origin.
After the 'run', nothing is clearly visible – photograph a. This indicates that a number of components, which are not coloured individually, can result in a coloured mixture.
Exposure of the thin layer to ultra-violet light reveals fluorescent blue spots – photograph b. All the spots are in the same position so they have the same R_f value – the distance travelled by the compound (as revealed by the spot) relative to the distance travelled by the solvent. The size of the spots reflects the dilution factor.
9a and 19 most probably have a common component. This would need to be confirmed by other means that employ different scientific techniques. Separation followed by infra-red spectrometry or by mass spectrometry or even an immune assay would be advisable.

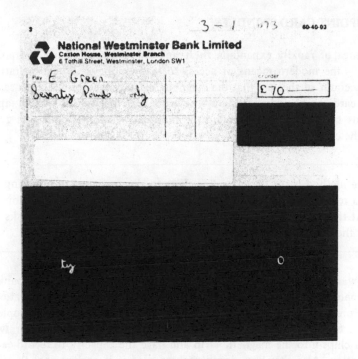

Figure 6.3 *Fluorescence beyond the red.*
The top picture shows a cheque in normal light. All appears to be in order and, no doubt, acceptable to the bank.
The lower picture is of the same cheque photographed when illuminated by light from the red end of the spectrum. Infra-red fluorescence indicates that two types of ink were used. There is no fluorescence from the 'seven' or the '7'. The 'ty' and the '0' do fluoresce and were apparently added at a later date. This would point to an addition by someone other than the signatory.
To multiply a meagre £7 by a factor of 10 is, in modern terms, mere 'peanuts'. However, had the original amount been £7000, the same few deft strokes could have put the final sum in 'the big league'.

Combined with detailed knowledge, and maybe a 'feel' for an Old Master, the laser is used nowadays to help detect an art forgery. A concentrated narrow laser beam is trained on to a pin point of the picture — usually in one corner. The paint materials are burnt off and the resulting vapour is analysed by means of its X-ray emission patterns. The constituents of the paint are identified and an approximate date ascribed to the painting. This can then be compared with the life period of the supposed artist. The spot from which the paint is burnt is not visible to the naked eye, so a genuine Old Master or a recent masterpiece is not ruined.

CASHPOINT CARD SWINDLES

One area of rapidly expanding theft and fraud involves bank cashpoint cards – the modern means of access to ready money. Shrewd operators take account of the fact that the magnetic message incorporated in a cashpoint card can be copied using a typewriter with magnetic ink on its tape. Various tricks are used to obtain the individual customer code that goes with the cashpoint card.

> One method is for the intending thief to ring up a customer, posing as a representative of their bank. He, or she, offers the information that the bank is changing its security coding and then casually asks for the present one. Usually it is given without question.

How did the thief come into possession of the names of the bank's customers in the first place? By way of an inside contact or by observation.

To prevent this easy access into the bank's reserves and other people's money, Smart cards have been devised. These incorporate one or two silicon chips into the magnetic strip and have the capacity to record each transaction. Also they can deactivate the card if it appears that there is misuse. Their complexity makes them difficult to copy but banks would have to change their entire cashpoint outlets to accommodate them.

Smart cards can, of course, be stolen and used illegally provided the user's code is obtained as well. The next development in the pipeline, designed to counter this, is to link the card and access to ready money to a personal identification. A voice-print could be in the records of the computer and money would appear only if the person quoted a given line from Shakespeare, or uttered a terse "Naff off!" A computerised visual recognition system called WISARD is being considered. In the bank's database would be a record of facial scanning of all the bank's genuine customers. In this case money would only emerge if the computer recognised the face after a prolonged stare.

Thieving ordinary credit cards and rapidly making use of them before the owner is aware of the loss is all too commonplace. The only real remedy is care and vigilance. Make sure that no one can lay his or her hands on a card or cards.

> Never leave a handbag in a parked car – even if it is locked.

In recent years the repertoire of those inclined towards unlawful activities has greatly been extended by the electronic revolution.

One young computer 'whizz kid' was put in sole charge of administering the salaries of a large multinational concern. Each month he deducted a few pence from the salary of every employee in the company. The deductions he added to his own salary. No one noticed. After several years he left and his replacement realised what had been going on. By then the trickster was well out of harm's way, basking on some sunny shore.

One ironic twist of the spread of computer corruption is that those who are caught, or admit to their misdeeds, are then put to use as security consultants – probably at a vastly increased salary!

A person who has successfully exploited a computer system must feel rather like the golfer who has holed in one – what is the use if you cannot tell someone? Many frauds involving computers are never revealed. Not only would public knowledge cast doubt on the bank's or firm's security, but insurance rates would rise with adverse effects on the customers.

The difficulty with crimes, or corruption, affecting electronic data storage and recall is that few ordinary people really understand what exactly is going on. Also those who claim to know have, with few exceptions, an air of detachment normally associated with the devoutly religious. To the large majority of the population the very word 'computer' causes a certain perplexity in the mind. In addition, this perplexity is frequently laced with apprehension. When a criminal robs a bank the sequence of events is obvious; forging a cheque needs no explanation. But computers are different and even among the young who equate electronics with games, the question arises "How is it done?"

SOME ELECTRONIC BACKGROUND

Fundamentally all electronic systems rely on the partial mobility of electrons in the atoms of a semi-conductor, like silicon. All electronic computing, particularly programming, is founded on the absence or presence of negative electronic charges. There are no half measures – either they are present or they are not. From this arises the binary, or two state, basis of computing. This quite simple state of affairs is also the basis of the relentless logic of computing systems, that many who operate them find so infuriating.

There are several stages to the setting up and operation of a computerised information system. The first is the input stage. Available data is transformed into its binary computer representation and placed on magnetic tape or disc. This stored data can be used for problem solving or simple recall. In recall the appropriate data is summoned on to a screen. With problem solving, a sequence of step-by-step instructions — the program — is required.

The information and the instructions are the 'software'.

The central processing unit of a computer directs operations and carries out the instructions in the program. This, along with the magnetic tapes and discs, is known as the 'hardware'. Hardware is, as its name implies, anything that can be kicked or attacked with a hammer.

The second stage is the output stage, where an operator at a keyboard terminal obtains information from the system. This output may be used by manufacturing firms to issue instructions to machines such as industrial robots.

Finally there is the transmission stage whereby the output may be communicated to users of other computers, sometimes at a distance from the source. Often this communication uses telephone, or similar, lines.

THE HACKER

Because of its very nature, hardware can be tampered with, but how can the software be broken into or accessed? Obviously, false input leads to unexpected or wrong output. Deliberately or otherwise, operators and programmers on the spot are often responsible for these false inputs. The hacker is not concerned with putting in information; he or she merely wants to know what is in a particular program. Sat in front of a terminal display unit, the hacker obtains entry to the store of information in a program from a distance. The end product of hacking is the required information on the screen. Somehow the hacker has to obtain the password into a particular program and this usually involves an inside contact. Many hackers, however, are merely passing the hours at their keyboards and 'log on' to computers more or less by chance.

> Apparently well over 50 per cent of computer corruption involves the staff that work in computer establishments. Software piracy is easy with a friend on the inside who works for a consideration.

It is possible to get round passwords by interpreting the computer's response to shrewdly worded requests. A computer cannot make qualitative decisions and so one way of wriggling past a password into a system is to find out how the computer responds by itself to the unexpected and maybe the illogical. A trained, intelligent computer operator can interpret these responses and find his or her way into classified information.

The communicating system, or network between computers, can be tapped by eavesdropping. Quite literally this means listening in to messages either by tapping the wires directly, or by picking up waves from the computer or its communicating system.

Any part of the hardware is vulnerable to those with violent intent. Sparks fly if the processing unit is attacked with an iron bar. The reason for such action can vary from sheer spite to utter frustration at this all powerful piece of human gadgetry. Computer operators evidently need an outlet for aggression, such as smashing a golf ball into the far distance or felling a tree with an axe.

Some employees, when dismissed from a company, have been known to instruct the computer to erase all the past records of the firm's transactions. Others in the same situation have made sure that the computer awarded them handsome severance payments.

The colloquial terminology relating to some computer corruption is, surprisingly, not an extension of the accepted jargon. Words, all charged with imaginative overtones, are borrowed from nature (such as worms and viruses), from mythology (such as Trojan Horses), from war (such as logic bombs) and from ancestral houses with a hint of secret passageways (such as trapdoors).

TRAPDOORS

A trapdoor is a way of sneaking past controlling passwords. A special portion is inserted into a program which allows the person inserting it to get at the information and instructions. While the presence of a trapdoor is known to the inserter it is unknown to other users of the system including sometimes the audit, or checking system. The question is, as always, who

91

inserts the 'foreign' program in the first place? The answer usually is someone on the inside.

TROJAN HORSES

A Trojan Horse looks innocent, as apparently did the original. It provides
the computer with acceptable information or instructions that in reality
contain hidden instructions that the computer can recognise. Authorised
users, without realising it, cause the hidden instructions to be carried out.
Once again an operator with privileged access must be responsible for
'wheeling in the Trojan Horse' in the first place. After performing its
purpose a Trojan Horse can — this time unlike the original — delete itself
so that no trace remains. This is a unique feature of gaining illegal access
to a computer.

> The machine itself can be programmed to obliterate all record of the
> intrusion. Does this herald the day of the 'perfect crime?'.

LOGIC BOMBS

A logic bomb is a device for causing disruption in the system. A signal, or
trigger, is incorporated into a program. When this section is reached in
normal operations, the result can be electronic chaos. The trigger may be a
particular time, such as 12.32 pm on 29th February, or a stimulus from a
remote control device. In any event a telephone call to a company inform-
ing the managing director that a logic bomb is in his or her computer might
itself trigger a heart attack. The erasure of records by a disgruntled employee is a form of logic bomb. Real bomb attacks have been made on
computer systems in the past.

WORMS

Computer worms, like the ones in nature, burrow. They originated because
someone noticed that most computers do nothing at night. What better
than utilise all that spare power for one's own purposes at someone else's
expense! In effect this means taking over the computer, or the computer
network, when the firm is not using it. Inserting a worm involves putting
a portion of a program into each computer that has spare time and linking

the portions together. When the main program is not working and the employees have gone home, the worm starts up. The separate portion in each computer is, appropriately, called a segment.

VIRUSES

A virus can be placed in the computer by some distant device, such as by instructions delivered by a telephone linked into the communications system. After migrating past the password, information is incorporated into the program. Like the virus in nature, this literally takes over and jams the system which grinds to a halt. The whole system is made to obey the instructions of the viral program, which is self-replicating. In effect a fatal computer 'flu takes over. Frequently, as with worms, a virus is set off at night.

In the computer sense viruses are malignant, worms are benign.

REMEDIES

In the face of this assault on the modern electronic system, what can be done? As regards both the computer and the communications networks, the answer might lie in more effective cryptography — the science of codes. Yet the experience of World War 2 showed that no code has yet been devised that cannot be broken. One recently developed code is technically unbreakable simply because of the time required to do so. Code breaking seems to have the same sort of fascination as solving crosswords. However life could be made much more difficult for the eavesdroppers.

The reduction of frustration, and consequent fraud, by employees seems to lie in the direction of tighter security and also in better staff relations. Tough passwords and sophisticated audit measures can maybe make accessing harder.

Gaining the cooperation of the staff would make everything more secure and this should perhaps be the top priority.

An emphasis on the welfare of people rather than the worship of machines might go a long way. The number of those who want to 'buck the system' would be reduced, although not eliminated, if each person

93

found some satisfaction at his or her place of work. It is an innate human tendency to want to step over the line that divides right from wrong. Even in the best circumstances that which is forbidden is attractive. So the sheer challenge of beating the passwords and manipulating the program will probably remain as long as computers are around.

7 The Electronic Arm of the Law

The prevailing attitude seems to be that "things are getting worse, no one is safe in their beds, let alone on the streets, and violence lurks around every corner." Something evidently must be done to make the place safe for law abiding citizens. So the police should be fully armed with all that modern electronics can provide in the way of information storage and recall, surveillance and communication.

> Two girls, both teenagers known to the author, suddenly decided to run off. They left notes and went. The parents, understandably, were distraught. They put the matter in the hands of the police, who quickly established that the girls had last been noticed leaving Waterloo station in London. One of the girls possessed a Building Society pass book and this was missing. The police visited the Society branch office and found that £200 in cash had been withdrawn. They requested that a message be put into the Society computer. This message would inform all branches that the girl's pass book number went along with a missing person.
> A week later the girl visited a branch of her Society and requested some money. The cashier noted the message and the police were informed. Both the girls were picked up just as they left the building. They were actually over 350 miles away from their starting point and nothing had been heard of them for a week. The message was subsequently deleted.

The main objection to giving unlimited electronic facilities to the police lies in the aspect of finality. It is not so much that the Police State looms with a thinly disguised Gestapo in operation. The root concern, voiced by those that support the movement towards Civil Liberties, is that modern electronic devices are considered to be infallible.

> The assumption is that the computer is right and there can be no appeal. No one queries the electronic 'bleep' at Wimbledon.

Experts know that mistakes are made by computers – in fact the whole system can be a victim of its own inner logic, as occurred in the Stock Exchange plunge of autumn 1987.

Firstly the input can be faulty, which is either the result of human error or deliberate malpractice. Secondly, background radiation such as cosmic rays, can cause random 'flipping' of negative electronic charges from one point to another. In a flash, ten thousand pounds in the black becomes ten thousand pounds in the red!

These chance events, however, can be detected using special codes but the problem is that no one really knows when they have taken place. The situation is more serious if a fault develops in the circuitry itself. Such is the fear and awe inspired by computers that such errors are rarely, if ever, admitted. A computer operates the Intoximeter mentioned in chapter 1. Its findings are not really questioned, although they can be checked by blood tests.

> In effect there is no doubt, just verification.

THE FINGERPRINT REVOLUTION

One of the most recent applications of computers is in the field of fingerprinting. The latest machines, known as second generation, are capable of scanning fingerprints, recording their characteristics and storing the information for recall when required for purposes of comparison. Whole fingerprints, portions of fingerprints and assumedly toe prints, can be scanned. It is claimed that the modern database is capable of receiving and storing up to ten million detailed instructions per second – a fact that defies the imagination.

> An entire fingerprint can be coded and stored in less than 4 seconds.

When recalling information for comparison with a suspect print, the existing first generation machines work at the rate of 1000 matchings, or comparisons, per second. Second generation models now being developed have increased this to 60 000. After a series of comparisons, a display of the closest matches are shown on the screen. The final decision is then a human one. An expert in this field claimed that sometimes a simple obvious match is missed.

Recording and storing the fingerprints of every child at school would be a simple, routine operation — no more difficult than mass vaccination. The implications for the future are obvious. The present manual method of comparing fingerprints, although time consuming, is efficient. When automation is introduced, as it will be, what happens to all those at present employed in the fingerprints departments?

DATABASES AND TRACE EVIDENCE

Information about the specifications and properties of materials such as glass and paint is invaluable. Both occur frequently as trace evidence. Often a suspect or victim is found with glass on, or around, his or her person. The point at issue then is — how does this fragment of glass compare with that taken from a vehicle involved in a hit and run offence, or that broken at a scene of crime? In statistical terms this becomes — what is the probability that the suspect and control samples come from the same source? This is *THE* relentless forensic qustion. Only patient scientific investigation can establish whether the two pieces have similar characteristics. If they do, are these similarities significant? It could, of course, be that the matching of the two pieces is entirely a chance occurrence. Statisticians, incidentally, like to talk about the probability of improbability and vice versa, which is most perplexing to the ordinary mortal.

To find out if the similarities are significant, the tests themselves have to be investigated. Were they on rare or on common characteristics?

Data supplied by the manufacturer and stored for recall on a database can yield this information quickly.

A match involving a rare characteristic is highly significant, because it is unlikely to occur at random. One involving a common characteristic is not so significant because any old two pieces of glass (or paint, etc.) could match in this way. Thus, if the match of the two pieces of glass is good and several rare characteristics are involved, then it is almost certain that the two came from the same source. This may, in the minds of a jury, put the issue 'beyond reasonable doubt'.

Rapid recall from a database is now standard practice with car ownership. Given the registration number of a vehicle, the owner can quickly be identified by contacting the computer at the licencing centre (DLVC) at Swansea.

WATCHING THE PUBLIC

Perhaps the major future use of electronics by the police is in the area of monitoring and controlling traffic. Even now the video camera and recording unit survey crowds at demonstrations, large riots and soccer matches. Fortunately the hallowed turf of championship golf courses has, so far, needed no such surveillance. In recent years the Americans have found that the protection of a President is most difficult during a casual round of golf. Keeping a close watch on acres of surrounding wood and countryside is next to impossible and the whole exercise resembles a full-scale military operation.

Efficient traffic surveillance ultimately means knowing where any car or lorry is at any moment of the day or night. This includes keeping track of stolen vehicles as well as those of wanted or undesirable characters. Into this latter group would fall suspected terrorists, political activists of the 'wrong' persuasion and anyone under suspicion.

It has been suggested that all vehicles should have an electronic signalling device incorporated into the chassis. At intervals on all roads would be a receiver, which would record the identity of all vehicles that passed over it. The whereabouts and route taken by a particular car could easily be traced. Soon cameras at traffic lights might be standard equipment. Those who 'jump the lights' will have their registration numbers photographed. At night the camera would switch to infra-red illumination.

On motorways, strategically placed radar or laser linked cameras could photograph speeding vehicles, or any other car etc. that might be of interest to the authorities. The essential point is that the photograph, like the computer 'read out', will be considered infallible. As one policeman put it:

> "It's more than a fair cop!"

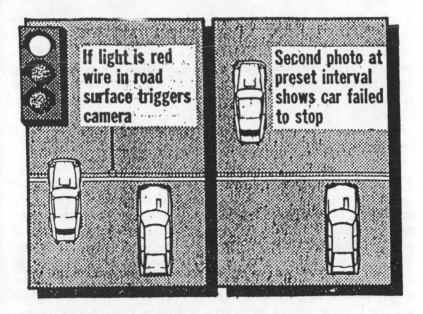

Figure 7.1 *The culprit at the lights.*
The eye of the law on the motorist. The important evidence is the photograph of the number plate of the offending vehicle.

Obviously there are benefits to the motorist arising from traffic surveillance. Knowing traffic densities at different times of the day in different places could ease rush hour problems. The police would have advance information on which to act and to keep traffic moving. Control after accidents would be more efficient. But traffic, and particularly crowd surveillance, means that innocent by-standers or passers-by are also photographed.

Would the fact that they are 'on file' or 'on database' affect these innocent people in any way? Should they be informed, or at least be able to find out if such a record exists?

Those involved with Civil Liberties want legislation to control the amount of information gathered about an individual and also the freedom of that individual to gain access to this information. The claim that:

"There is no need to worry if you have nothing to hide."

is small comfort to a person who has been refused a passport and is unable to find out why.

The means of collecting information is a matter of concern also. Photographs are perhaps allowable. But what of telephone tapping and opening mail? The more these things are done the more they become accepted and acceptable.

MONITORING CRIME

When the facts of all reported crimes in a given area are fed into, and processed by, a computer, a crime density pattern (similar to a traffic density pattern) can be built up. This helps with the efficient deployment of manpower, particularly when resources are low. The situation is similar to that of the Battle of Britain. Radar, then in its infancy, gave accurate information about the direction and weight of attacking forces. Accordingly the fighters were able to intercept at the best place and time. The alternative, as with policing, was to maintain constant patrols over a large area, which was, and is, costly on men and machines. Whether the occasional, or even regular appearance of a foot police patrol is reassuring to the aged and infirm is perhaps open to doubt.

When a crime is committed and reported, it is possible for a computer to scan the m.o., or *modus operandi*, files of habitual offenders. This could indicate the most likely candidate to interview — probably much to his or her surprise! If a crime is committed by a newcomer to the criminal fraternity, the computer is stumped. However, the situation would be different if there was background data on everybody — fingerprints, voiceprints, blood groups, DNA fingerprints, all of which are inherited and last unchanged for life.

The investigation of a major crime, or series of crimes, committed by one person is helped by the use of a computer to process information. Some claim that the Yorkshire Ripper would have been caught sooner if the computer had been employed to scan, store and match the facts of successive rapes and murders.

In the USA, computers are now being used to reach out into the future in a 'predictive capacity'. At the National Center for the Analysis of Violent Crime, a team is working on compiling a database that will, hopefully, enable the authorities to take action before a crime is committed. It really involves seeing into the mind of the criminal and predicting intent.

People well established in the public eye — stars of TV, politicians, sportspeople — are sometimes the target of 'stalkers'. These individuals idolise a famous person and follow him or her around the States — hence the name 'stalker'. Eventually this pursuit culminates in an assassination attempt. In the case of John Lennon, this attempt was successful. The fear of these predators in the crowd has prompted some of those at risk to turn their opulent residences into virtual fortresses. One motive of the 'stalker' is perhaps revealed by the comment made by Ronald Reagan's attacker. When taken into custody his immediate concern about the incident was "Is it on TV?"

In order to counter this menace, the security men have now been joined by the 'threat assessor'. A 'stalker', according to those who know, shows 'self-announcing' patterns of behaviour and 'predictive indicators' of intent. More often than not these are detected by a close study of fan mail letters, particularly a series from one individual.

Information from suspect letters is selected by the assessor and placed on the database of the computer at the National Center. When sufficient data is available it is processed and then scanned. The results are interpreted by a specialist – usually a psychiatrist. When a certain pattern becomes clearly recognisable, the author of the letters is visited and removed from all contact with society and the target celebrity.

Whether this represents an over-optimistic use of electronic resources remains open to question.

VISUAL IDENTIFICATION

A large part of criminal identification has, in the past, involved artists building up impressions from the statements of witnesses or victims. This was, and still is, somewhat time consuming as is the inspection of a pile of photographs to see if 'that's the chap'.

Electronics experts have recently developed EFIT, a process whereby bits and pieces (eyes, ears, nose, etc.) of facial features are recalled from a database. A face forms on the screen when these bits and pieces are fitted together. This face can be modified by altering the various components until a witness or victim claims a good likeness to a criminal or attacker. The final impression can be stored and communicated to police forces around the country.

A further system, known this time as FACES, uses a database that stores information obtained by scanning the photographs, or 'mug shots', of known villains. Instead of thumbing through books of photographs, the victim or witness studies a screen on which the faces appear. If none of the pictures can be recognised as the criminal or attacker, then the face bearing the closest resemblance is altered in its detail to give an exact likeness.

This final 'fit' is then put into the database for future reference. In both these systems — EFIT and FACES — the aim is speed and accuracy.

THE QUESTION OF BALANCE

Inevitably the use of new technology in a sensitive region such as crime prevention and detection leads to questions. When misdemeanours are recorded and placed on a database, is the weight given to each item the same? For example, is a youngster caught scrumping apples automatically classed with the GBH character or the gold bullion thief? In days gone by those in the first category merely received a sharp thump round the back of the head and were told not to do it again. Needless to say, the response was to take better precautions against being caught next time. Nowadays a minor incident in youth could mean that chances of employment or promotion are blocked.

The very fact that one's name, or photograph scan, appears on a police database, albeit accidentally, implies some measure of guilt.

The respect, adulation almost, accorded to the modern computer, or anything electronic, makes this conclusion impossible to avoid.

Yet there can be benefits.

The author, his wife and family recently visited a hotel in the country for a celebratory dinner. The wine and food were excellent. The bill arrived and was found to be some £40 short. In response to a polite comment concerning this discrepancy, there was an immediate affirmation, "That's what the computer says." In the circumstances it was considered unwise to press the point further.

THE RIGHT OF ACCESS

A further question is — what right of access should the police have to inspect an individual's records on other storage systems? For that matter what are, or should be, the rights of access of any authority? How available should be an individual's medical records, employment records, educational records or financial records? One suspects that such files or databases are accessed surreptitiously. The issue is one of personal privacy and the familiar claim of 'nothing to worry about if there is nothing to hide' does not entirely allay the fears.

As in all things, there are maybe crumbs of comfort. The grim era of the highwayman came and went. Now it appears that the bank robber is about to bow out. This is simply because there will soon be no hard cash in circulation. The flourish of the sawn off shotgun, the stocking over the face and the barked warning to get on the floor will all be in vain. The vault and the till will contain computer tapes, 'print outs' and nothing else. The fiver and the tenner will have become redundant as all financial transactions will be conducted by cards of some description. Bank and train robbers of the old mould will be forced to stay at home watching television, drawing social security and bemoaning the 'good old days'. The forgers will have to look elsewhere or go out of business.

One consequence of entrusting to the forces of law and order the full might of electronic wizardry, is to accelerate the trend towards central control. The immense costs involved mean that duplication on a regional basis would be more than extravagant. The National Police Computer (NPC) at Hendon is the present centre of a network that can be accessed by any regional police authority. Some feel that this is Big Brother in the making. The disadvantage of automation and technology tends to be the enhancement of the 'us' and 'them' mentality. So much information so readily available is alarming to the ordinary soul. As one person aptly expressed it:

"Soon they'll have more on me than I know about myself."

8   The End of the Line

Having assembled all the facts, what does the forensic scientist do then? What is the point of establishing connections between suspect and control items? To what end has all the time and effort been devoted?

The next, and final, step is to submit his or her findings as evidence to a court of law. Sometimes the evidence is written down and read out during court proceedings. At other times the scientist is required to enter the witness box and present his or her observations and results as verbal testimony. This means that the evidence, and in fact the scientist, can be tested by cross-examination. This often entails answering searching questions.

Science plays a much greater part in crime than it did, and so science has to be employed on an increasing scale by the investigators. The modern forensic 'detective' often lives in the commuter belt, is likely to sport a Ph.D. and to write papers for scientific journals.

THE EXPERT WITNESS

In court the forensic scientist is given the status of an expert witness and, in consequence, is liable to be asked for opinions as well as facts. Only experts are asked this; the ordinary witness must stick to the facts. Also, as an expert, the scientist usually represents a team. He or she cannot possibly carry out all the experiments and observations alone. So the scientist can present evidence that has been established by others working under his or her supervision. This is a kind of hearsay, which is allowed because of the complex nature of modern science. Normally hearsay, which is best illustrated by

---

"Sid told me he saw Joe stab Fred"

---

is not admissible in court.

The expert witness, whoever he or she might be, must appear credible. This is a matter of appearance as well as qualifications. In order to avoid comment or even thinly disguised ridicule, it is advisable to play along with the system. Dress smartly, try to appear relaxed, never lose one's cool in spite of provocation and do not rate too highly one's part in the proceedings. Try to strike a serious, professional attitude. When taking the oath speak clearly and, if possible, with conviction. Even though few people may actually believe in God or the Creator, the oath is important. Deliberately making a false statement under oath constitutes perjury, which is itself an offence. Also statements made under oath have, like those made in Parliament, absolute privilege. This means that no one can be sued for such a statement.

As an expert witness, the forensic scientist must be strictly impartial. He or she is no one's advocate. Within the laboratory practice of forensic science itself, stringent precautions are taken to ensure that the objectivity of the scientist is maintained. The work of the scientific officers — the Forensic Service is part of the Civil Service — is regularly checked by their seniors. Training is rigorous. As has been indicated, a system of Quality Assurance applied within the laboratory means that any individual scientist is periodically given 'blanks' and 'unknowns'. This keeps the wits sharp. The scientist is aware that this is likely to happen but does not know when. If possible, suspect and control items from the same case, such as two garments, are inspected in different parts of the laboratory.

THE CORONER'S COURT

Forensic evidence to a Coroner's Court is usually given by a forensic pathologist, who is a specialist of the medical profession. Coroner's Courts deal with those already dead and forensic pathologists are responsible for carrying out autopsies. These are done in hospitals although some of the samples collected from the body may be sent to a forensic laboratory. A Coroner's Court is convened to carry out an inquest. If a body is found and circumstances point to death by unnatural causes, the Coroner holds an investigation, or inquest. The aim of this inquest is to identify the deceased, establish the place and time of death and, if possible, find the cause of death. A Coroner is obliged to hold an inquest into a death resulting from a road traffic accident or the death of a prisoner while in custody.

THE MAGISTRATE'S COURT

Evidence by a forensic scientist can be given in a Magistrate's Court and in a Crown Court. Magistrate's Courts are in effect the filter system of the legal process. When a charge is laid before a person, he or she is first brought before the Magistrates. Prior to this appearance the Crown Prosecution Service will have established if there is a *'prima facie'* case against the accused. *'Prima facie'* literally means 'at first sight', but in a court of law it means a 'reasonable' or 'genuine' case to answer. Sometimes the Magistrates are asked to confirm this *'prima facie'* case. If the offence is serious (known as an indictable offence) then the Magistrates carry out committal proceedings for trial by jury in a Crown Court.

Less serious, or summary, offences are usually brought to a conclusion in the Magistrate's Court. The aim is to avoid wasting the time of Higher Courts. Most Magistrates, or J.P.s, are lay people but they must undertake initial and on-going training. A stipendiary Magistrate is a qualified barrister. In Court the Magistrates — there are usually three — sit on the 'Bench' and are addressed as 'Your Worship' or as 'Sir/Madam'.

THE CROWN COURT

Crown Courts, the modern equivalent of the Assizes, reveal the full majesty of the law. Robed judges sit on 'the Bench' and are addressed as 'My Lord'. Barristers, or counsels, acting on behalf of the defence or the prosecution of the accused, take their place 'at the Bar'. The jury — twelve ordinary men and women — sit facing the witness box. The setting and proceedings of a Crown Court are designed to impress all present that the Law and its representatives are to be respected, if not feared. What the actual effects are on the person in the dock must remain open to question.

The responsibility of the forensic scientist, when called to the witness box, is to present clearly the facts and how they have been established. After cross-examination, he or she may leave the courtroom and perhaps never consider the case again. Pressure of work normally prevents a scientist following a case through to its conclusion. In fact it might not be wise to do so. Yet even the most dedicated and detached person is affected by events around them. When specimens are presented for examination after a major riot, no one can avoid the impression that this is 'red hot'. However, under no circumstances does the Forensic Service wish to be considered as a weapon used by the police for its own purposes. The scientist in the laboratory is interested in who pulled the trigger, not in proving that the accused actually did so. In some cases the forensic evidence has compelled the police to release a suspect.

NATURE OF FORENSIC EVIDENCE

Most forensic evidence presented to a court of law is circumstantial. This means that it is concerned with the circumstances arising from an offence. Blood on a garment, marks on a window frame, fragments of glass in a roadway are all circumstantial evidence.

Inferences can be drawn from this type of evidence to link an individual to the scene of the crime. These links are important when members of the jury consider their verdict. The judge, in his or her summing up, draws attention to the relevance of these links. Frequently, circumstantial evidence is the only evidence available. There is no direct evidence of the offence. Modern photographic and electronic gadgetry are providing more and more direct evidence of offences. Videos are now standard equipment on business premises; infra-red cameras record vehicles 'jumping the lights' at night; financial transactions involving drugs can be recorded if the apartment is appropriately 'bugged'. Whether the evidence of these recording devices is admissible is decided by the judge.

The best direct evidence is visual

> "I actually saw Joe shoot Sid"

although this is admissible only if the speaker or writer is regarded as credible. The words of a proven liar — even if they happen to be true — carry little weight. Yet even honest, well intentioned people vary in their interpretation of the truth. The evidence of several direct witnesses of the same incident often shows surprising variation.

THE NATURE OF THE SYSTEM

According to one officer of the Court, constructing courtrooms and expanding prisons is now one of the major growth industries in the UK. The Law is big business — its turnover could well approach that generated by large-scale crime. Both — crime and the Law — thrive together rather like the symbiotic union of two gigantic organisms. The judges who sit on the Bench and the barristers that hold forth at the Bar wield considerable power. A person charged with an offence can, if found guilty, be deprived of freedom for many years and can be detained at 'Her Majesty's pleasure' in positive discomfort. The previously mentioned officer of the Court put it in a nutshell:

> "It's all a big game really. Designed to protect the interests of the ruling classes."

TRIAL BY JURY

The purpose of a court of law is to establish guilt or innocence. Normally in a democratic society this is achieved by submitting evidence to a jury. They assess the facts and reach a verdict. If two expert witnesses disagree, it is the jury's task to decide between the various versions. They might reject both. The process of trial by jury is centred around the adversarial approach to justice. Advocates argue the case for the defence and for the prosecution. Both try to convince the jury by persuasion and reason, with the odd appeal to emotion. The spoken word is the very foundation of the jury system of justice. Consequently those with a facility for verbal fluency and rapid thought thrive at the Bar. Barristers readily acquire such arts because success depends upon it. The scientist, essentially a practical man or woman, may not be a master of the language with a fine turn of phrase and a quick wit.

For some reason, known only to themselves, a jury may occasionally acquit a person against whom the evidence seems conclusive. What goes on behind the closed doors of the room where the jury deliberate is never revealed. Strictly a verdict must be arrived at without any outside influence – only the facts must be considered. The judge can give a clear indication of what is expected in his summing up. However attempts have been made – successfully in some cases – to 'nobble' members of a jury. This simply means that pressure is applied to a particular jury member or members in order to obtain a certain verdict.

When a powerful and influential member of the criminal fraternity appears in the dock, his minions in the outside world have ways and means of exerting pressure. Promises of rewards or unpleasant consequences ("we know the route your nipper takes to school") can do much to cloud judgement. After a trial when terrorists have been convicted and found guilty, the jury may need police protection for some time afterwards.

THE FUTURE

The jury system is infinitely better than trial by torture, or by ordeal, or by the whim of a dictator. In addition there are channels for appeal in order to redress miscarriages of justice. There are, of course, limits. Constant appeals would bring the system to a halt. As yet nothing has been devised by man to improve on trial by jury — or even to replace it. But there are signs.

The results of the Intoximeter, on which breath alcohol levels are determined, are taken as final and virtually infallible. Attempts to cast doubts on the Intoximeter findings are stubbornly resisted. The recent development of DNA fingerprinting can be applied to paternity testing with a probability that is 99 per cent certain. In the future this technique could be applied to cases of rape, assault and murder. The validity of the charge "That man raped me!" could rest on one scientific test. At least, intercourse could be proved if not rape itself.

One quite revealing fact has emerged from the practical application of DNA fingerprinting/profiling. It is now used to establish the credentials of people wishing to settle in the UK. In the past the existing blood grouping systems — ABO and Rhesus — indicated that many, perhaps a majority, of those claiming to have a close relative (father, son, etc.) living here were not telling the truth.

The more accurate scientific test involving DNA shows that a high proportion — some claim over 90 per cent — are in fact making a correct claim. This may point to the fact that people (at least the humble ones) are more honest than they are given credit for — an embarrassing conclusion for those of a cynical or ambitious nature!

Trials are proceeding with a camera linked to a radar device operating from a stationary car on the side of the motorway. The radar device detects any car that is speeding and the camera records its registration number. The replacement of the radar device with a laser would improve the efficiency. Duplicated photographs (one being sent to the owner) would constitute the only evidence needed for a conviction. In fact, the stationary car need not be manned by any police personnel.

The system of trial by jury with scientific evidence as a contribution might change to one of trial by science with the jury fading into the background. Determined opposition would be expected from the legal profession, who would be alarmed at any erosion of their power and influence. Even the scientists might object, although several have commented wryly, "There is no justice in a court of law; there isn't even a search for the truth; only a scramble for a verdict." No one, however, is perfect and scientists have been known to draw conclusions from inadequate or insufficient results.

THE SENTENCE

> The author's grandfather was called for jury service once in his life-time. With eleven others he witnessed the awesome spectacle of the black cap being donned prior to sentence. The accused went to the gallows.
>
> Doubts always remained in his mind but in those days no one dreamt of questioning the directions of a judge. These doubts were reinforced when later a man confessed to the murder on his death bed.

After the verdict, just or otherwise, the final act of the courtroom drama is the sentence handed down by the judge. Frequently these are made public and many a scientist, or ordinary citizen, has been surprised at the sentence delivered. There are guidelines but these are not made known to the public who go on a kind of rough common sense.

Sentencing perhaps becomes less puzzling if one considers the observations of an experienced barrister. He posed the question: "Apart from offences that carry a mandatory sentence, such as murder or treason, what offence is likely to lead to the stiffest penalty?" One obvious reply was, "Stealing from the rich." Close – but not close enough. The offence most likely to bring down the full wrath of the Bench is one that is committed in the vicinity of a judge's residence. Breaking and entering in East Ham or Bermondsey might just raise a few legal eyebrows. But put a foot wrong in Belgravia or lift the odd tenner from the locker room at Sunningdale and the reaction is swift – provided the culprit is caught. Not only are the sentences stiff but the storm of indignation from the Bench leaves the offender in no doubt of the enormity of his or her crime.

The last word, in all fairness, must come from the lips of a Lord Chief Justice in person:

> "In England justice is open to all. But so is the Ritz hotel."

9 Crime and the Citizen – a Personal Perspective

From the strictly legal point of view, a crime is an offence against the law. It is not surprising, therefore, that those who formulate the law stand to benefit most by it.

Offences are classified according to their effects on individuals, property and society.

> The worst crime, it is said, is simply being found out.

Many, however, appear to revel in the publicity of being apprehended and the prospect of a spectacular trial. Confessions from 'nutters' are not uncommon after a gruesome murder or devastating fire.

The general public does seem to have its own ideas about the importance of certain criminal activities. These ideas often contrast quite sharply with the intentions of the law makers.

HOW MUCH CRIME ACTUALLY IS THERE?

No one really knows the true extent of a particular offence or of crime in general. Statistical studies are based entirely on offences that are reported to the police and thus appear 'on file'. All else is speculation. Reporting for some offences is higher than for others. Most insurance companies now require evidence of police involvement before paying up. But, according to most authorities, a vast number of incidents go unreported. The recent increase in the number of reported incidents of rape may reflect a greater willingness on the part of women to report the offence. This, in turn, may reflect a changing attitude on the part of society in general and the police in particular. There may be no more rapes than before; in point of fact there may be fewer. No one knows for certain.

The facts show that violence to a person by someone unknown to the victim is quite rare. In the sanctity of the home it is different. Males, females, young, old and infirm are at any time likely to bear the brunt of physical violence when passions run high. But then it has always been so. At one time, life itself was described as 'nasty, brutish and short'.

IS THERE REALLY A CRIMINAL TYPE?

An acquaintance of the author had a sixteen year old son. This young fellow was quiet, smart of appearance and pleasant of manner. In fact he was an exemplary middle class, reserved youngster with no thought of transgressing the law.

Suddenly he decided to 'get himself a crew cut'. His habits did not change as he stepped from the hairdresser. Yet within the space of ten days he had been stopped and questioned by the police three times.

His mother was furious.

ARE THERE 'ACCEPTABLE' AREAS OF CRIME?

1. No one doubts that moving vehicles on the road are responsible for death and destruction on a substantial scale. Yet, despite the hard facts and the Christmas campaigns, there is still a reluctance to regard motoring offences as really serious — unless you are on the receiving end! Deterrence comes largely from the inconvenience of being without a licence rather than from any concern for other road users. There are perhaps signs of a change of attitude. Motorists are taking more care and a device has been developed that is a DIY breathalyser attached to the ignition system of the car. Not only does it satisfy curiosity ("am I over the limit?") but if the exhaled breath is above the 35 μg% deadline then the car is automatically immobilised.

Being 'picked up' on the road is often a proud boast and exhaustive accounts of brushes with the law on the highway are guaranteed to liven a dull party. Recognition has always been given to the chap who can hold his liquor and the motor car confers masculine status. This means that driving with more than the legal limit of alcohol (ethanol) in the blood is 'acceptable' to some sections of the community.

> One young blood used to proclaim loudly, "If I find my car parked crooked in the garage I know I was sober when I drove it there. If it is perfectly straight then the chances are that I was drunk when I got home." He was not joking!

Speed is, or can be, most exhilarating. It is the easiest thing in the world to top the ton on a near deserted motorway. Maybe "clearing up human mess off the roads" — as one policeman put it — is just another fact of life.

2. White collar 'acceptable' crime is conducted on the quiet by seemingly respectable people. Large-scale fraud or insider dealing may not have public approval, yet most people, with more than an even chance of success, cannot resist a fiddle on the side. Ordinary souls (the author included) who would not dream of stealing from an individual, would not hesitate to do 'Them' down — particularly if 'Them' happens to be the Inland Revenue. Shoplifting, a different proposition maybe, is now classified as big business. Large stores cover themselves by adding to the price of their goods. Ironically, if the store detectives are efficient, the end product is increased profits.

3. Some kinds of 'acceptable' crime actually approach the artistic. Forging tickets for the Centre Court at Wimbledon or Cup Final tickets for Wembley demands a level of skill and dedication that prompts admiration. Of course 'acceptable' in this context means that you have not been sold one of the forgeries. It could be that the forger of modern art devotes more time and skill to his work than the artists do on the originals.

The attitude towards computer hackers or electronic manipulators is frequently 'good luck to them'. In the USA, smart operators who have accessed highly secret electronic systems have ended up at the White House being congratulated by the President — and being photographed by the FBI for future reference!

THE UNACCEPTABLE FACE OF CRIME

Most public concern is generated by crimes of violence against the person and property. The prevailing mood is, by all accounts, one of increasing fear. Some people do not venture out for fear of attack on themselves or their empty houses. People have returned from holiday to find their entire house cleaned out by thieves. The market for safety devices booms as never before. Affluence is maybe not all that it is cracked up to be.

While not denying the claim of public fear, it must be borne in mind that if people are told often enough that they are frightened – they usually are. Researchers have pointed out that those who feel most at risk – such as the old age pensioners – are actually in less danger than other sections of society, notably young men under the age of thirty. Often when put to the test, the old show remarkable courage and some recover from quite savage attacks.

A young student alighted from a coach at a large terminus. It was a bright morning with only a handful of people around. She waited for her connection northwards. Suddenly an arm came round her neck and she saw the flash of razor blades between the knuckles of a closed fist.
"Your purse."
She groped for the purse and held it up. Before he could grasp it he was struck a violent blow across the back of the head.
He relaxed his grip and ran off empty handed. She never saw his face but turned to thank her rescuer – a determined old lady swinging an umbrella. How many men would have done that?

The difficulty with violence is that the issues are not clear cut. Rape, murder, assault and vandalism generate disgust in reality but make for excellent television. Drug abuse is nothing like so dramatic and makes little impact on the casual viewer even when woven into a highly popular soap opera. Hooliganism on the soccer pitch or picket line violence is fascinating, particularly when viewed from the safety of the lounge with a can of ale within grasp. The thin blue line holding its own against mass pickets or a horde of soccer fans on the rampage ensures high viewing figures, which is just what the media want. After all some people – women no less than men – scream for blood at boxing matches.

THOSE AT THE RECEIVING END

Recently a branch of study has opened up called Victimology and this could, in time, influence public attitudes. It examines the effects of crime on victims and the issue of compensation for injury and damage. Also it addresses the thorny problem of whether there are individuals who 'ask for it'. In legal terms this is known as contributory negligence, of which the best known example is not wearing a seat belt.

Women complain about the attitude that a young lady dressed to attract the opposite sex actually invites an assault. Criminals claim that the ostentatious display of worldly wealth — Old Masters hanging in full view over the mantlepiece or diamond necklaces scattered around the bedroom — means that the owners are almost pleading to be relieved of their treasures.

According to the experts there is really no defence against the determined, skilled professional. Alarm systems, dogs, electronic gadgetry can all be taken out. Only neighbourhood watch schemes make much difference and frequently the enthusiasm wanes with success.

The author's late uncle, who farmed rich acres along the Kennet Valley, became the proud owner of a brand new Humber Super Snipe, in the days (the early 1950s) when such cars were difficult to come by. The fact that his land adjoined that of the Managing Director of the Rootes Group — manufacturers of Humber cars — might have been significant. They shared a pheasant shoot that stretched over both farms.

One day he drove this plush new automobile to a far pasture and parked it in a gateway beside the road. He locked it and left both his dogs inside. These were fully grown black Labradors and were fiercesome animals at the best of times. In his car they became positively ferocious at the approach of a stranger. He strolled across the meadow to inspect some cattle and returned to the road. The car had been out of his sight for no longer than 10–15 minutes. He found both dogs drugged and dumped by the roadside. The car was gone. It eventually turned up, battered and stripped down, in London. The thieves were never caught and the police were baffled by the speed and efficiency of the theft.

One redeeming feature of this incident was the fact that the dogs were spared. Modern criminals would probably have shot them out of hand.

A LAST THOUGHT

Attitudes to crime, like everything else, probably depend much more on personal experience than on rational considerations. If you have had your home burgled then, in your eyes, crime has never been so bad (despite the fact that the insurance payments were more than generous) and the entire country is fast going down the drain. However, if your neighbour — the one with all those rowdy dogs that make such a din in the night — has his place done over, then you really cannot see what all the fuss is about. In the end one can only go about one's business relying on luck or the grace of God according to one's inclinations.

Index

118

119